AF423794

SHUT YOUR DONUT HOLE

A guide to building confidence
while being your magical self

KATIE KRAMER

For **YOU**….

The woman who is reading this and questioning her worth…

You are here to do amazing things.

More importantly, **YOU ARE ENOUGH**.

Don't forget it.

Contents

FOREWORD

There are two things I have been doing my entire life: eating donuts and writing. I blame my mother for the donut addiction. Her food of choice when she was pregnant with me were warm glazed donuts, so I feel I came into the world with glazed donut DNA. As far as writing goes, I've always loved writing and have taken every opportunity I could to get my thoughts on paper and into the hands of others.

Confession: this isn't the first book I've written. My first book ever was a beautifully illustrated little number I called *The Christmas Cat*, which I wrote for my parents back in grade school. It was about a cat with a red and green striped tail that covered it so no one would tease her or notice she was different. Now, as I look back at that short book (yes, I still have it), I see it as foreshadowing for this book and who I was meant to be. The artwork may have been amateur level, but the message: timeless. Never be afraid to stand out or be different. As Drake said, "You don't worry 'bout fitting in when you custom made."

I've always been someone who marched to the beat of her own drum, but there was a **LONG** time where I tried to ignore it. I'm sure you have been there, too. You may even be there right now! It's a place that I truly believe we all spend some time at in our lives, and no one can convince me otherwise. It's exhausting to be anything but yourself, so if you are struggling with that, I am so glad you picked up this book. We're going to work on this together!

Who is this book for exactly? This book is for you if you are:

-Trying to live the life you "think" you need to in order to please those around you.

-Trying to make decisions based on what you "think" others would want you to do.

-Dulling your sparkle to fit into some boring box that you "think" is the way you have to live.

-Letting others dictate how you are living your life in any way, shape, or form.

-Aren't loving or appreciating the wonderful uniqueness that is **YOU.**

There are a few things I want to make sure we cover before I start sharing what I have used to regain my confidence over the years and to find the courage to be my genuine, weird, and authentic self 24/7. When you are struggling to find confidence and figure out who you are, it is common to justify certain thoughts and beliefs as they make sense to you.

As I was gaining confidence and starting to feel really good about the person I had become, I started telling myself things that would justify my thought process. This is exactly how my way of thinking aka Katie Logic came to be. Remember how Carrie and Big came up with their own rules for marriage in the second *Sex and the City* movie? The Katie Logic rules I'm going to share with you are basically the same thing….my own rules for living my best life.

A quick Katie Disclaimer because we all know I need to come with one, and this book is no different….

For starters, I am not a therapist or any form of counselor, nor do I want to be. I am just someone who has weathered many storms and has worked really hard to overcome some challenging times. Life is a crazy thing with no instruction manual, and our problems are not one size fits all. I don't pretend to have all the answers or have my life together, but I do know that the things I am sharing in this book helped me in some way, especially with gaining confidence and learning to love the person I am, so if they help someone else I consider this book a huge success. I am very confident and proud of the woman I am, and I want every person reading this to be able to say the same!

It is important for me to share with someone just getting acquainted with me that I cuss. I cuss a lot. More than a sailor, actually. I will not apologize for this, nor will I feel bad for using colorful language. This is just who I am!

As I sat down to write this book, it was important for me to write as though we were having a conversation between two friends. I wanted you to read this and feel comfortable with me at my realest and rawest, and sometimes that is a lady who needs her mouth washed out with soap or makes her mother cringe a bit. It is also important to state that apparently there is a pretty strong link between profanity and intelligence, so I'll just leave you with that for now. However, if a good ol' fashioned F-bomb bothers you,

you can always turn back now and skedaddle over to something a little tamer.

My goal for this book: to get **YOU,** the beautiful majestic sunflower reading this book, to realize that your mouth is meant to speak positive, uplifting, and kind words about yourself and that you are meant to live life on your terms. Ever hear the saying, "If you don't have anything nice to say, shut your donut hole?" Ok, that may be the Katie version, but it is the same as just limiting the negativity coming from your mouth. Stop the negative self-talk, stop the self-sabotaging actions, and start replacing the thought process of needing to please others with pleasing yourself first…...preferably with a glorious sprinkled donut in your hand.

I'm always rooting for you.

XoXo,

Katie

THE TWEENER CHAPTER

Before we completely jump in, I want to take a moment to get you into the headspace I was in when I needed to make some drastic changes in my life and give you a little more background on who I am. You can't understand how I am **NOW** without understanding the earlier stuff, so this chapter will be the bridge between the then and now. Let's hop into our DeLoreans (big movie fan over here) and hop back to the summer of 2013.

If you were someone just skimming the surface of my life, maybe just seeing the highlight reel I would post on social media way back then, things looked like they were pretty freaking amazing. I had worked in higher education for a little over a decade, allowing me to hold some amazing positions at various colleges. This was important to me after all the sacrifice I had put in to get my Master's Degree completed in just under a year and a half in my mid-twenties. That thing cost me a lot of money….I had to put it to use! I was (and am still) very fortunate to have a great group of friends all across the country, which allowed me to travel and have a pretty full social calendar. However, there were more internal battles and struggles going on within me than people realized.

Behind the scenes I had just broken away from a tumultuous on-again off-again relationship that had been mindfucking me for the better part of six years, a relationship that had served as the springboard for a very unhealthy relationship with alcohol and fast food. It was the kind of relationship where nothing I said or did was ever good enough and one that came with more insults and negative talk than anything. My self-esteem had completely gone into the shitter, and I believed very little in who I was and what I could offer. While I believed very little in myself, I was somehow able to believe all of the awful things that would come out of his mouth.

Only one friend in that during that time frame had actually met him, and because of this, all of my family and friends who hadn't were not members of his fan club. When I **FINALLY** gave him the pink slip for about the hundredth time, I slowly started to retract from the things I loved so I could stay at home and hang out with the one thing that never disappointed: my White Russian. Her friend Long Island Iced Tea was a frequent guest as well. We were quite the team.

I've been very open on my social media platforms about the struggles I had with alcohol, and even to this day it amazes me how well I hid some of them. I remember clearly the first time I came out and shared with everyone that I was an alcoholic and had gone to Alcoholics Anonymous meetings. My mother said to me, "Your drinking really wasn't that bad," and I remember telling her, "Mom, it's because I didn't let you know how bad it got." I was **SO** good at hiding what I was doing, as many of those battling an addiction are. I can't believe the lengths I would go to when it came to hiding my love of alcohol and the chokehold it had on me.

I often took those mini liquor bottles to work in my purse for moments when the day got "rough". My evening routine had become one where every night I would come home from work and down six or seven large White Russians, drinks that were twice, sometimes three times, the size of those you would get at a bar. I would drink them until I passed out on the couch, get up, go to work, and repeat the cycle. When I wasn't drinking I was thinking about it, and when I was the next drink I was planning on having was already on my mind.

I had fallen into a place where drinking was the only time I felt peace. I felt safe at home with my drink each night, watching reality tv and eating the fast food I had picked up on the way home. I told myself I didn't have time to work out or cook or anything else, yet I always had time to drink. I made excuses for everything except for the alcohol. The alcohol would **ALWAYS** win.

The person I saw in the mirror was not someone I was happy with, and it wasn't until one morning when I was trying to get ready for work that I realized how far gone I truly was. The only pair of pants that still fit me in my closet would not button, and I disguised a pair of yoga pants as the bottom of my business suit that day. I cried and thought, **"WHO IS THIS PERSON?"**

I had gained almost seventy pounds and felt so lost and ashamed. Later, in a drunken hot mess state, I purchased a workout program bundle that most of us see late at night on infomercials as we try to fall asleep. I had no clue what I had done until the box arrived at my doorstep a few days later.

Fortunately, during this time one of my friends, someone who lived close by and had seen my decline, was waiting at my apartment when I came home. She was there to stage an intervention with me and take me to my first AA meeting. It was terrifying, humbling, and everything I needed. I was angry at her, yet thankful. The emotions I felt with her interference into my life are feelings I could never describe in words. That night I committed to getting help and began the road to sobriety, attending countless meetings in my area and using my new-found online fitness community to give me the extra support I needed to make healthier choices and focus on something other than alcohol.

I will not sit here and tell you those early months were easy, because they were anything but. I avoided social situations that may compromise the lifestyle I was working toward, was terrified to share about my new fitness journey online for fear I would be judged or made fun of by my peers, and refused to open up about what I was going through with my family. It wasn't that I was afraid they wouldn't support me, because I knew they would. It had to deal with the fact that I didn't want to be a disappointment to them or embarrass them, and I feared telling them about my alcohol addiction would do that. As someone who had always been a "good" kid and overachiever, I was terrified what opening up would do to how everyone would perceive me, especially my parents.

Back in those early days I learned I needed to find some kind of substitute to make me feel good so I wouldn't see alcohol as my only "feel good" option. Insert fitness here.

I started a home fitness program truly believing I would not be able to do it and would quit. I **KNEW** I would quit. In my head I contemplated what I would do when I failed this program. What would my next failed attempt be? That's how low my self-esteem was. I had zero belief I could do anything.

Yet, as I did my first workout, huffing and puffing and modifying every move, I felt more alive than I had in a long time. The former college athlete in me was back, and I slowly started to believe I may be able to do it. "I may really be able to lose some of the weight I had gained," I would tell myself after I finished a workout. The best part: I was feeling happy and so good each day I got that sweat session in.

In addition to working out following a structured program, I had plugged into an online fitness community of strangers who helped me stay accountable, and I actually found myself really going all in.

As I went to AA meeting after meeting, my workouts became that one thing I could rely on and that I needed every single day to feel good, and they kind of took over that place alcohol held in my life. I looked forward to them every day. Each day that I would check off the workout on my calendar I felt like I was one day closer to a better version of me. It was a glimmer of hope each day that I desperately needed.

I wrapped up the program I started ten weeks later, and what a day that was. I cried because I had finished, then I stepped on the scale and cried because I had lost just over forty-seven pounds during that time frame! My diet had been modified somewhat, but I wasn't following a set meal plan, just eliminating fast food and processed foods while still living a sober lifestyle, so no alcohol. Above all, I felt **AMAZING**.

Guys, I was **SHOOKETH**.

I remember that moment when I stepped on the scale and how I felt like it was yesterday. It wasn't just about weight loss, even though I knew based on my poor health losing weight was a must due to my medical history. I knew I needed to get healthier because of my decline, but as happy as I was to finally be out of the "morbidly obese category" (Yes, at the time I fell in that), I was just so proud that **I DIDN'T GIVE UP**.

I have goosebumps as I write this because it was one of those **A-HA** moments in my life. It is still one of those moments in my life that I could tear up when thinking about it; it was truly that impactful. Have you ever heard the Mark Twain quote, "The two most important days in your life are the day you are born and the day you find out why?" That day when I stepped on the scale and felt that feeling of accomplishment for seeing something through I realized my why.

Proving to myself that I could get back up…. that I could rise after being knocked down so low….and to get amazing results strictly from good ol' fashioned exercise and support…. I wanted to help everyone I could get to that place. I knew the stats and that obesity was at an all-time high, and I knew that there were so many women out there like me, struggling with inner demons that were keeping them from living their best life. Some women were closet alcoholics like I was. Some were coming out of awful relationships, while others were just struggling with their self-esteem.

Even though I was a long way away from where I wanted to be self-esteem wise, I knew I had just proven to myself that I could do something with the support of others, and I wanted to be that support for those women out there that needed it. I wanted to make a difference. I wanted every woman to have that moment I had when I got goosebumps after stepping on a scale and realizing **"HOLY SHIT**, I did this!"

From that moment on, I decided I wanted to go all in with health and wellness consulting, helping to connect other women out there to the same supportive online community that helped me and a variety of fitness programs that could help them based on their needs. I knew very little about network marketing, but I did know that I was incredibly scared of what my friends would think. Will they make fun of me? Will they support me? Will they talk behind my back or say I am part of a cult or scheme? Alllllllll the thoughts ran through my head, and for a while I let them get the best of me.

It took me almost five months, but I finally struck up enough courage to post my before and after photos from that first online challenge online. I remember hovering my finger over that enter button for almost an hour, so scared of posting those images. And then, I did it. I pressed the enter button….followed by me sitting there with tears in my eyes thinking, "What did I just do?"

Quickly all of my insecurities about posting unflattering photos of myself...all of my fears of saying the word "alcoholic" in a sentence…all of the trepidation of sharing how poorly I felt about myself…….vanished. Comment after comment was posted, sharing how I was a source of inspiration and motivation for those reading my post. Friends were excited for me and proud of me. The support and encouragement I received was unbelievable. I couldn't believe how good it felt just sharing what was truly going on in my life, and to know that others supported me and were cheering me on. It was a vulnerable moment, but so authentic and genuine.

I realized in that moment a very important lesson that I have carried with me ever since, a lesson so powerful that it kicks off our first chapter and will forever serve as the foundation of being a confident, strong, and powerful human being. Ladies and gents, it's time to learn what Katie Logic is all about.

Katie Logic #1:
FUCK WHAT THEY THINK

Yep, kicking it off with an F bomb because that's how strongly I believe in **THIS** statement. You read my disclaimer, right?

Of all the things I have learned over the years, this has been the hardest to learn, the hardest to practice, and the hardest to be consistent with doing. Regardless of what we discuss or work on when it relates to becoming our best selves, everything always **COMES BACK TO THIS**. This is what I like to refer to as "The Cardinal Rule of Confidence!"

If only one thing sticks with you after reading this book, please let this be the one. **PLEASE!** It is by far the most important, which is why we are discussing it first. Why? I am convinced that **OTHER PEOPLE** are the biggest reason why we don't pursue our dreams, why we don't believe in ourselves, and why we spend so much time second guessing things that we do. Prove me wrong. Go ahead, I'll wait.

The town I am from, a small town south of Youngstown, Ohio, was the type of town back in the day where everyone knew everything about everyone. My high school had about four hundred people in it, and that included junior high, with my graduating class at just over fifty people. It was such a small town that we didn't even have a stoplight or blinking light. Needless to say, in a town that size it is kind of challenging to figure out who you are when you aren't surrounded by many people and where "different" really isn't a thing. The term "cookie cutter" comes to mind. It was a beautiful town, safe, and a great place to grow up, and I am so thankful I was able to experience it, even if it did come with its own set of challenges.

I feel very fortunate because two of my absolute best friends in the world have been in my life since early childhood. We grew up together, graduated together, and have remained close as adults. I love them for so many reasons, but the biggest reason: they have always loved and supported me for **ME**. Neither ever made me feel I needed to be any certain way at any point in my life, and for that I thank them.

I can't say that other individuals during my high school and those impressionable years acted the same. I remember feeling like I wasn't cool enough because I wasn't wearing a certain kind of jeans to school, and it wasn't because I couldn't have them, it was because I thought they were ugly with a patch on the ass. Eventually, I gave in and got a few pairs so I could fit in. That's what happens when you are young and impressionable and want to be included.

My younger self was a weird person. I didn't really want to wear makeup or rock a hairstyle other than a ponytail, and a fly outfit to me included a Scottie Pippen jersey and a pair of basketball shorts, which paired perfectly with a pair of Converse sneakers. I was gangly and for a time wore glasses with a red frame before making the jump to contact lenses. Like a normal teen, I had some sweet acne on top of being just awkward AF.

I'm sure I definitely came across as an introverted bookworm type, but the truth was I just didn't know how to share who I was yet. I was scared of how people would judge me if I was louder or shared more of my blunt personality, and for that reason, I held a lot in. You could say I was a rule follower, and a big part of that was because my parents set clear expectations and rules for my brother and I. I did not want to deal with the consequences or do anything to negatively impact the big goals I had for myself.

I differed from most high school kids because I was very focused on getting good grades and playing sports, and because of that I didn't want to be involved in the party scene like many other young kids who are curious about alcohol at that age. One of the very few times I did attend a high school party, it got busted, resulting in a multi-game suspension from volleyball for all of the players in attendance, which crushed me. It just wasn't something I was interested in, and I still remember **NOT** wanting to even go to that party, but going just because the guy I liked was going to be there.

I think back to my earlier days as I was figuring out who I was and try to recall a specific incident or person that made me feel I needed validation from other people, and to be honest, I can't recall one. Deep down, I just wanted to fit in and not be made fun of, which is probably what the majority of teenagers would say. When you lack self-esteem, you don't want to do anything to rock the boat or draw attention to yourself, so I just went with the flow of what others were doing, even if I did not like it.

Now that I am older and wiser (or so I think), I see newspaper articles that say women "should be (fill in the blank) or (fill in another blank)" and magazines that say we should weigh a certain number. I watch shows that glamorize certain things and create a materialistic mindset that makes those watching feel like that's the only way to be. I see apps on social media to distort our appearance, reshape our bodies, and all kinds of other weird things. We are to blame, people, we as a society! I hear it all the time whenever I drop an F bomb or other colorful words that are laced in my daily vocabulary. "Ladies shouldn't speak that way." Excuse me, but can you take a moment to go back in time to reference where it says how a woman should and shouldn't act? Again, I'll wait.

Coming from a small town, it was challenging to be the person I was for so many reasons. My town had an old-fashioned mindset and everyone seemed to fit inside the same box, and that's hard when you are trying to find your place and voice in the world. It lacked diversity, culture, and open mindedness. How should I talk? Is my hair weird? What kind of attire is cool? Should I wear a glitter bow in my hair or would that look strange with my basketball jersey? Will I have to sit by myself at lunch? All of these were questions that would come up in my mind.

My love for all things sparkly started when I was a very young child. Believe me when I tell you that I was born with glitter in my veins. I truly think I was. I have gravitated toward sparkle my entire life, and it now has an even greater presence in my life, as it serves as the mission statement for my business. What started as a love for glittery hair bows has now become a way of life for me.

My mission: to leave a little sparkle wherever I go. Why? I believe we all should leave others better than we found them and share a little bit of our own individual sparkle with everyone we meet. My role on this planet is to share my sparkle and make a difference, and it is the mission I remind myself of daily. If you think about it, that's what we all are hopefully doing. We all have our own unique sparkle that can benefit someone in some way.

I remember an incident in junior high when I was given an incredible pair of multicolored sequin shoes from my grandparents for Christmas, and I couldn't wait to wear them to school. I wore them the first day back from winter break and remember how excited I was to march into school with my sparkly feet. My excitement and the happiness they brought me quickly diminished when a few girls in my grade made fun of them and subsequently me for wearing them. I cried in the bathroom so they couldn't see me in such an emotional state, fearful that it would give them another reason to be mean to me. I couldn't wait to get home to take them off. The worst part of that day: I remember how incredibly sad I was because I loved them so much and felt I shouldn't wear them anymore. I didn't wear them to school much from that point on and wore them at home instead. I'm sure my dogs loved the sparkle they brought to the living room when I would prance around in them.

I wish back then I was brave enough to have defended myself and feel proud of my shoes. Those shoes…. those were Katie shoes if I have ever seen a pair, and to this day they remain my favorite shoes of all time. They were (and still are) such a representation of me. Everyone back then….and I mean **EVERYONE**…. rocked a particular brand of plain white sneakers (so not me), and those were deemed to be the "it" shoe and status symbol of cool. It's hard to be a sequin shoe in a world of plain shoes. You feel me?

As we get older, so many of us still deal with that insecurity of wanting to fit in and please others. It's almost as if the junior high version of us is still trapped inside and afraid of having to eat lunch alone. We become wiser with experience, we become more confident with the things we like, but we **STILL** focus on other people's opinions. Why? Do other people's opinions make you happy? Because they sure weren't making me happy back then. If we are being honest, I can't tell you a time when other people's opinions on my life choices **MADE** me happy. I was living my life for others, not for me.

What makes you happy? Like seriously every single time you see it/wear it/think about it you get the warm fuzzies and could squeal with excitement? That's the shit you need to bottle up and put on blast.

This is the part where I tell you that I really like list making, and I find it so incredibly helpful as one embarks on a personal growth journey like you are about to be on. At the end of every chapter is a space for you to write down your answers to the things I ask, like the things that give you that warm fuzzy feeling I just mentioned. You want to write these things down to bring light to how awesome you are and help you grow through this book, as well as give you something to reflect on as you progress with your confidence journey. I like to call these "self-love scribbles."

Yeah, I'm obnoxious about donuts...they are pretty much my favorite thing…. tied with all things glitter of course. Does that make other people roll their eyes? You bet. One time I wore a sequin skirt to the grocery store on a Tuesday just because it made me feel good, and the cashier said "Kind of overdressed to buy avocados." My response: "This is just how I live my life." That's a fucking fact, Jack. I didn't think about what I had to do that day when I got dressed; I thought about how I wanted to **FEEL.**

You don't have to like sequins or anything sparkly for that matter, but they make **ME** happy. I don't care what kind of craptastic day I am having. I put on something sparkly and I feel like I'm walking down a runway and **I AM HERE FOR IT**. It's the runway called **LIFE**, motherfuckers, and I'm going to own that **EVERY. DAMN. DAY.**

There was a time where I would've thought sequins were too bold for a Tuesday at the grocery store. Who made up that rule? Probably someone who was scared of being who they were and afraid they would get teased. Sequins get you out of your comfort zone…**GOOD!** You have to get outside of those comfort zones to really live life. So many things we love or could love are sitting right outside of our comfort zones, but we are too scared to pursue them. We are lying to ourselves about what they mean to us or how badly we want what is out there because it is just easier to go with the flow and stick with the familiar.

You know who goes with the flow?

Dead fish. Don't be one.

I challenge you to do something super bold and out of your comfort zone that aligns with whatever your definition of happy is. Put on something fun you love and just wear it to the dog park. Who cares what other people have to say! Dress to impress, and I don't mean impress others. Dress to impress **YOURSELF**. Does it make you happy? Do you feel good? Yes? Then that's all that matters. Do your makeup in a way that makes you happy. Dye your hair that crazy color you've been wanting to do. Just chase down happiness, friends.

I'll tell you something big. When I made the decision to cut ties with what other people thought of me and who I was, my stress and anxiety levels went **WAY** down. I knew I was living an authentic life, I wasn't pretending to be someone I wasn't or trying to fit it. It was me, take it or leave it. It gave me such a feeling of freedom I had never experienced before, not to mention the feeling of being powerful that came with it.

While my stress and anxiety levels decreased, guess what increased? My overall happiness. I felt good. I felt happy. And above all, I felt like I was being myself….my true self, and that is a feeling that is unmatched. It's powerful to know you aren't letting people rent space in your mind, not to mention that you are experiencing a new level of happiness because **YOU** found your own way to it by your own authentic choices. There's a quote I once read from Dita Von Teese that just stuck with me, and I think about it often. She said "I've always loved the idea of not being what people expect me to be." **PREACH IT, SISTER!**

You've got to look at yourself as an acquired taste. Not everyone will like you and want to be around you, and that is okay. You might be too much for some people (not your people). You might not be enough for others (still not your people). You do not want to water yourself down to be what others want. You want to be the person that at the end of the day **YOU** love when you look in a mirror. It is liberating to know you need **ZERO** validation from anyone on this planet and that **YOUR OPINION is ENOUGH**.

But where does it all start? It starts from realizing who you are, learning to love that person, and being confident in how you live your life every single day, and that's not easy.

So how do we do that? Let's dive into some more Katie Logic and work on it, ok?

Chapter 1
SELF-LOVE SCRIBBLES

What makes you happy and gives you the warm fuzzies?

Chapter 1
SELF-LOVE SCRIBBLES

I'm proud of myself for getting out of my comfort zone by:

STOP PLAYING IT SAFE

"Alexa, give me Confidence!"

Wouldn't it be cool if we could just speak those words and suddenly have all the confidence in the world? Confidence is not something you can just demand on the spot, or even something you can just suddenly have one day.

Whenever I'm having a conversation with someone about pursuing a dream or finding the motivation to do something, there usually is some kind of obstacle that comes up, and it is usually a person in their life. I call these people energy vampires and dead plants, and you better believe we will be talking about them a little later on.

Remember what I shared earlier? Everything comes back to the concept of **FUCK WHAT THEY THINK**. This is truly where confidence begins to grow because you are coming into your own as your very best version and most magical self.

People that meet me now always assume I have always been the loud, confident, and strong woman I am today. Oh, child, let me tell you. The old Katie…. man, did she question every single thing and every single thought and every single decision, even when I was starting to come into my own as an adult. I'm here to tell you….confidence is **NOT** something that came easy to me. Confidence takes **WORK**. Developing rhino skin takes **WORK**. Even our cardinal rule of **FUCK WHAT THEY THINK** (FWTT for short) takes work. If you meet someone uber confident, know they weren't born with it either. They put in a lot of work to get to that place, whether you know it or not, and they are **STILL** working on it each and every day.

When I revisit my own stroll down Confidence Lane, I would say my own confidence didn't even begin to surface until I left for college. Most of my early life I played it safe. Coming from a small town, if I messed up even in the smallest of ways, **EVERYONE** knew about it. I never got a detention (not even a lunch detention), and the first bout of trouble I got into was my junior year in high school when some friends and I got caught shoplifting at a Sears. I'm not even going to get into it, but we were idiots. It was a matter of hours and **EVERYONEEEEEEEE** knew about it. I tried to avoid being a part of the rumor mill as much as possible.

The most dangerous thing you can do in life is play it safe, and it doesn't matter what stage you are at in your life. You have the opportunity every single day to throw out the rules and establish new ones. Why aren't you doing it????!!!!!

I know, I know…. you're just waiting until you are done reading this book so you are better prepared, right? I like how you think.

Let's talk about a few "play it safe" rules that I think most of us have fallen victim to in our day. Probably the biggest: I should go to college and get a degree. A close second: I should be married by such and such age and have kids by (insert child birthing deadline here). A third: I shouldn't do that because no one else is. Any of those sound familiar? Been there, done that for all three of those. Who are we trying to please by adopting this "play it safe" mindset? Clearly not ourselves.

I don't regret the decision to go to college one bit. This was a time where I was able to spread my wings and start to develop into the person I am today, and I'm very thankful for it. It provided me with great friendships, great experiences, a great education, and a super attractive student loan debt upon completion of my Master of Arts degree. That was what I should've done, right? According to everyone around me, the answer to that was yes.

I'm sure if I told my parents I didn't want to go to college, they would have been supportive had I had some kind of plan, but I know they wanted me to go, and I'm not even saying I **DIDN'T** want to. I just thought that I should, end of story, and because of that didn't pursue any other option or give anything else serious thought. Deep down, I wanted to pursue a wrestling career because I was (and still am) obsessed with professional wrestling. I had the height, I had the attitude, I knew how my costume would look (sequins of course), but what would people say if I pursued that over a degree? There was **NO CHANCE IN HELL** that would fly.

Then there's the marriage thing. I was **LITERALLY** one of the last of my friends to get married, and I didn't get married until the age of 34, only to get divorced not long after. Crazy as it sounds, I am thankful I went through this at the point in my life I did because if I was younger, I probably would not have walked away or done anything to change the course of my future. We shouldn't divorce, right? Only losers do that. That just shouldn't be in the thought process….at least my younger self would've thought that.

And who wants to go against the grain and do something that no one else is doing? That's just a terrifying thought, especially when you have zero confidence! When I made the decision to jump into my health and fitness career full time, people thought I was crazy. I wish I could share screenshots of all the messages and DMs I got asking me why I would leave such a great career in higher education to do "some pyramid scheme". I even had people accuse me of falling off the sober wagon, asking if I had started drinking again and made an impulsive career move as a result of it.

I'll tell you why:

1) Because I wanted to.

2) It made me happy.

3) This is my life, and it isn't a dress rehearsal. I've got to make every day a day that matters, and that is why.

4) Fuck what you think.

Playing it safe and having a lack of confidence are basically besties. We struggle with our own conviction, thoughts, goals, and desires, and we are scared of being made fun of, talked about, questioned, etc., so we play it safe so no one ever does those things. Have you ever thought that your **LACK** of conviction or pursuit of your dreams can cause others to talk about you the same way chasing those dreams and carving your own path in this world would? If you are adopting the FWTT mindset, that doesn't matter because #fuckwhatithink, but if you are just starting out getting brave enough to embrace this mentality, we need to switch up your thought process for a second.

Seriously **THINK OF IT IN THIS CAPACITY**: Every single thing you are doing is drawing a response from someone out there...maybe a family member…maybe your spouse…. maybe just an internet troll, so why are you just not doing what makes you happy? What about the response from **YOURSELF**??!!!! That's the only response that matters, sis!

It baffles me that I spent so much of my life searching for approval from others, and right now you may be doing that, too. That validation that we are "doing the right thing" gives us the confidence to do something that maybe in our hearts or in our gut doesn't feel right. But...someone told us it was the right thing to do, so that should be good enough, right?

I can't tell you how many times I knew what the right thing to do in my life was, but I just wasn't brave enough to do it because I didn't want the headache/ridicule/questioning (insert whatever negative you want to attach to this here). My own inner happiness was always pushed to the back burner because I just wanted to avoid any of that uncomfortable stuff. Sometimes I want to go back to that younger version of Katie and shake her silly!

Back to confidence and how we can start building ours…….

Let's talk about three steps that I feel are important for you to implement right freaking now to get that confidence moving in the right direction. If you don't have a highlighter, grab one…. some parts of this book you should want to highlight in addition to scribbling out your answers to the things we discuss at the end of the chapter.

STEP ONE: Realize that confidence is a muscle that needs work every single day. **EVERY FREAKING SINGLE DAY.**

You didn't wake up one morning and suddenly bench press three hundred pounds, did you? Nope. You spent weeks and months and maybe even years at the gym working on those muscles every day, increasing the weights little by little until you hit that goal. Confidence is the same! You don't just wake up one morning this majestic She-Beast that walks confident AF. You work on it a little every day, increasing that confidence and self-love little by little until you get to the level where you have rhino skin and are living out the FWTT mentality every damn day.

Are you someone who makes a daily list of chores and things to accomplish? If so, add this to your daily To Do list. I'm serious…. write down "Love my damn self" or "Work on my confidence" right there under picking up your dry cleaning or groceries. I'll say it a little louder for the people in the back: it has to be a thing that happens daily!

STEP TWO: Get real with yourself.

Make a list of all the things you like about yourself and all the things you have to offer this world. Don't tell me you don't have any, because the lie detector will determine that is a lie (Shout out to Maury Povich for an iconic line that I use way more than I should). This may be hard for you to do, but I want you to try. I want you to also write a separate list of all things you struggle with or the areas where you lack confidence the most. These are things that cause you pain and could also be referred to as pain points. Is it body image, and the thought of wearing a crop top makes you want to cry? Is it going up to a guy you think is cute at a bar and introducing yourself? Is it posting a video on your social media because you are self-conscientious about your voice and how it low key sounds manly? Hi, I had this issue, so if you struggled with this, know I feel ya.

Identifying these things will help us work on them. Want to get to the next level with this? Ask someone close to you like a spouse, close friend, or sibling to share the things they love most about you. If you are struggling with coming up with anything, this will help get the thought process in motion! Write as many things as possible down.

STEP THREE: Write out a list of affirmations.

For those of you not into affirmations, let's chat about those really fast. Affirmations are statements that begin with **"I AM"** and you fill in the blank with something you want to become the truth. Honestly, they are more of a declaration of what you want to become a reality. These statements you should look at daily/weekly (whatever frequency you want to and need to), and speak them into existence. Does that sound a little crazy? Maybe. I definitely thought so the first time this topic came up to me.

Me: Why the heck am I going to sit at my desk and talk out loud to myself about something that hasn't happened yet?

I definitely said that to myself more than once, and if you are saying it now, that's okay. Welcome to the Affirmation Skeptics Club, and I think the majority of us have all had a membership for a while. I may have even held the President role in that club for a hot minute.

Here's the thing with affirmations: you read them, you speak them, you start to believe them. I had the same ten affirmations every single day that I would not only read daily, but write down in my gratitude journal, too. I still have them memorized to this day because I said them and wrote them for so long. This practice became just part of my morning routine and also a time to set my intentions for the day.

Something about when I stated those affirmations helped me to complete the tasks I needed to work toward obtaining those goals. They helped me focus. They motivated me. They helped me visualize them coming to life and happening. They made me believe I could **DO** the things I was saying. Once you start believing and taking action to make that affirmation a truth in your world, big things happen. Trust me on this.

Take some time right now to jot down ten affirmations you want to make a reality. If you have more than ten, that's okay, but identify the **TOP TEN** as far as importance. I had lots of goals the first time I sat down to write mine, but there were ten that I identified as the ones I had to chase down first.

Want to know the first one that was on my list?

It was this: "I am a published author."

I always knew I wanted to publish this book, but I had so much to say and so many directions I wanted to take it that I just played around with the thought for way too long. There was a point early on where part of me lacked the confidence to follow through because I didn't think anyone would want to read a book I wrote other than my mom.

Now?

SO WHAT if my mom **IS** the only person who reads this. I wanted to write this to fulfill a personal goal I set for myself and to make good on a conversation I had with my father years ago where I told him someday I was going to publish a book. I said I was going to do it, and I did the damn thing. Yaasssssss, girl!

Always, always, **ALWAYS** write down your list of affirmations because sometimes just seeing it on paper makes what you are writing click. The first time I ever wrote mine down I put them in the notepad on my phone. You can always start there because I know you have a cell phone #facts. In addition, writing down your affirmations is forcing you to get real with yourself, which brings us to another piece of Katie Logic….our bullshit.

Chapter 2
SELF LOVE SCRIBBLES

What are ways you can work on your confidence daily?

The things I love about myself include:

Chapter 2
SELF-LOVE SCRIBBLES

The things I struggle with the most and areas where I lack confidence the most include:

In what ways are you "playing it safe" in your life?

Chapter 2
SELF LOVE SCRIBBLES

My Ten Daily Affirmations:

1.

2.

3.

4.

5.

6.

7.

8.

9.

10.

"I AM ENOUGH."

OWN UP TO YOUR BULLSHIT

Your bullshit or your growth? There is **NO WAY** you can get out of your own way and grow if you don't commit to one of those.

Yeah, I said it. You have bullshit that you have been feeding yourself. We have all been there, friends! One of my favorite quotes ever came from Elizabeth Gilbert (I have so many favorite quotes if you haven't noticed). She said, "I've never seen any life transformation that didn't begin with the person in question finally getting tired of their own bullshit." Truer words have never been spoken!

What kind of bullshit am I talking about? The lies we tell ourselves to make things seem okay. This could also apply to anything we do and say that helps us justify a decision to do or **NOT** do something. Bullshit is the stuff that is preventing us from truly being our best version of ourselves. If right now you are sitting there thinking… "Hmmm, would x,y,z be considered bullshit?", then just ask yourself if it is helping you grow. If the answer is **YES**, then it's not bullshit. If the answer is **NO**, guess what….it is. Own up to what it is, and don't sugarcoat it. It's freaking bullshit.

I go back to when I was at rock bottom #1 in my life. It was August of 2013, and I was a **HOT MESS**. Actually, scratch that...my friend Jess and I determined we are more the "spicy disaster" type because it has somewhat more of an appealing ring to it. I lied to myself for way too long because I didn't want to face my own bullshit. It's hard to say "I need help." Sometimes it is just about trying to save face, too. I didn't want my own bullshit to impact the lives of those around me, even though it was without me knowing it. Eventually the bullshit became too much for me to handle. I was drowning in it.

At that time, I had a great career, but that's really all that was going for me. I was in a relationship with a raging alcoholic who lied and cheated and was just awful to me. As I mentioned earlier in this book, it was one of those on-again off-again things where you are basically being mindfucked the entire time. My self-esteem had been shattered over the six years that was going on.

"He can be really nice at times," I'd tell myself. I sidelined the nasty comments he would make to me, the fact he never felt the need to meet my family or friends, how he always "forgot" about my birthday or other major holidays, and the fact that numerous people had found him on other dating websites while we were together. My friends all hated this dude and constantly were trying to get me to see the light. Honestly, I do not understand **WTF** I was thinking back then. It took me a long time to realize what kind of emotional abuse I had dealt with during the time I was with him.

My dedication to working out and maintaining a healthy lifestyle had completely disappeared, and I had gained about seventy pounds in the process. Beyond that, my alcoholism was out of control. I would rush home from work every single night to down as many White Russians as I could, and alcohol ruled my thoughts. On days where I was just so overwhelmed, I would drink those mini bottles of alcohol at my desk at work in secret, which was basically every day because my job came with so much stress. I **ALWAYS** had at least one of those in my ginormous oversized purse **JIC** (just in case). "Everyone does this though, right," I'd say to myself as I poured another drink. Hello, that is me trying to justify my bullshit.

The breaking point came that one morning when I went to get dressed for work. I had entered my huge walk-in closet that was loaded with clothes, and not one pair of pants fit me. My "fat pants" (ladies, we know we all have them) were my last hope, but they, too, did not fit. That was the day I went to work wearing that pair of yoga pants disguised as a suit bottom with a blazer over top of it. When I got home from work, it was immediately time to drink, as I was ready to indulge in the White Russians I desperately needed to get past the stress of the day. That was the night I drunkenly purchased the home workout program I mentioned earlier, the night I signed up as an online coach (to save money so I could buy more booze), and also the last night I would spend shitface wasted.

Unbeknownst to me, the next day after returning home from work, I would find a friend of mine at my apartment with a goal in mind. She was sick of seeing me self-destruct and was staging an intervention. I had thought I had hidden my behavior so well, but I hadn't hidden it from her, and she was scared for me. I went to my first AA meeting with her that night, and it became the start of a sober lifestyle.

That day I saw through all the bullshit I had been telling myself. I couldn't get healthier because of x,y,z. I should give my ex a chance when he called because maybe he had finally changed.

Alcohol was always the answer…. blah blah blah. Looking back, I can't believe how much bullshit I had fed myself.

I sat in my apartment shortly after that first AA meeting and made a list of all the bullshit I had told myself. Things like "This is the relationship I've always wanted" were included. Katie, **WTF?** A piece of scum that literally provided nothing good or positive in my life….who made you an option when you made him a priority...who called you a fat fucking bitch on a daily basis…that is what I always wanted???? No, girl. **NO.** Literally the ONLY nice thing this person ever did for you was take you on a ghost tour **ONCE**, and he bitched the whole time about how lame it was. C'mon, Katie. That boy's picture is next to the word bullshit in the dictionary.

I was at a point of settling because I was playing it safe. I was past the age of 30. I should be married by now….and that thought process of thinking about what others saw to be "normal" was contributing to the bullshit I was feeding myself. On top of all of it, the biggest piece of bullshit was me telling myself that **I WAS THE PROBLEM!** I constantly told myself that I was why the relationship wasn't working out. Katie, **WTF?!** I **DEADASS** believed I was the problem and the root of all of the nastiness that went on during that time frame.

Bullshit…. it's a dangerous thing.

What about your bullshit? What bullshit are you feeding yourself? Let's do a simple exercise to figure that out if you aren't sure.

Sit down and write out all of the goals/dreams you want to accomplish or fulfill in the next year. Be specific. Then write down the reasons **WHY** you have not accomplished them yet. Don't be vague either. Get **DETAILED**. The more detail you write down, the more bullshit you are identifying in your life. You need to get it all out. If you are really trying to work on your confidence, and I **MEAN REALLY WORK**, you can't just half ass this confidence journey. You have to full ass it!

Those reasons why…. guys, that's your bullshit.

Be real with yourself. I know, I know…. sometimes that is hard AF. You can't change if you just stay the same. Growth happens when we look at the pieces of ourselves that aren't their best and work to actively make them better. You have to get out of the way of your own bullshit!

Here's a little truth bomb: We are **ALWAYS** going to have some kind of bullshit creeping into our lives that we try to justify. As I type up this chapter, I currently have a situation going on with someone in my life that I low key caught myself trying to justify. The difference with owning your bullshit as your confidence increases and you become more secure in who you are is that you really become solid at identifying it, knowing what you deserve (and don't deserve), and taking out the bullshit trash.

Back in the day, I justified everything as "that makes sense" or some other convoluted weird ass explanation. I now see it for what it is, and once you identify it, it become easier for you to work quickly to combat it. That bullshit will do nothing but

BRING YOU DOWN. Don't work so hard on yourself only to fall back into those old ways.

Speaking of growth and bullshit, **BE BRAVE ENOUGH TO OWN UP TO YOUR MISTAKES**. One of my biggest areas of growth, which ultimately is tied to confidence, is owning up to the massive amounts of mistakes I have made. And yes, many of those mistakes are tied directly to the level of bullshit I fed myself.

Here's the thing, friends. We **ALL** make mistakes, some of us a shit ton. Some of us don't even realize in the moment we are making them that they are mistakes or will come back to haunt us in the future. We are living in the moment and perhaps uneducated or just plain ignorant to something we are doing or saying. Are our intentions harmless? Probably. That doesn't mean we gloss them over and don't own up to them if they do come back to bite us in the ass.

There's a whole different level of confidence that comes forward when you tie it to accountability. It takes balls to hold yourself accountable, especially when it comes to a mistake that maybe had a negative consequence and experience attached. It takes balls to take responsibility instead of pointing the finger and blaming someone else. It takes balls to say, "My bad, I'm sorry, my fault." Do you realize how challenging it is for some people to say "I'm sorry?"

Know what else it is doing? It's giving you control of your life, your actions, and your future. It's showing you are confident in who you are and all your imperfections. Above all, it is showing you are ready and willing to grow as a human and be better than you were yesterday. That's really all any of us can do, right?

We are living in a time that is really challenging, and it just really bothers me. It seems like every single day someone is trying to be combative and attack someone else for a decision or action or statement they made. It's like so many people thrive on seeing others get punished or cut down. Everyone assumes something has an underlying tone or negative meaning, and it just makes me sad. When did we get to a place in society where we sought out the bad in every person, not the good? And when they apologize never really let them live it down? It makes my heart hurt.

People make mistakes. I make mistakes. You make mistakes. **EVERYONE MAKES MISTAKES**.

Own up to your bullshit when you do…. take responsibility for your actions…. stop blaming others….and feel much more in control of your life.

Capiche?

Chapter 3
SELF-LOVE SCRIBBLES

What bullshit am I currently feeding myself daily?

Chapter 3
SELF-LOVE SCRIBBLES

What goals/dreams do I want to achieve in the next year? Why have I not already accomplished them?

STOP WATERING DEAD PLANTS

You need a tribe. It doesn't matter how old you are, where you live, or what you do. You need to have a pack of people who can be those cheerleaders that lift your spirits when you need them to but also celebrate you like crazy for just being you. I want people in my life that will always have my back and who will also leap out of the dugout with me if I ever decide to charge the mound.

I feel very fortunate to have the people in my life that I do who cheer me on and love me for me every single day. They love me at my best and love me at my worst, and I never ever have to apologize for who I am or how I am. That's fucking friendship.

I mentioned earlier in the book that I am very lucky that two of my best friends in the world have been in my life since we were little kids. I'm talking about preschool times, people. That means they have been my friends for **DECADES**. They've seen all the hairstyles, they have celebrated amazing life moments, they were there when I got married, they were there when I got divorced, they were there the moment I found out my dad died, they are just **MY PEOPLE**. There are periods of time where we don't talk for weeks or sometimes even months, but whenever we do get a chance to talk, it is like a moment never lapsed from our last conversation. They are my ride or dies, and I'm thankful for them more than words could ever say.

Over the years I have added to my close inner circle, and while **BFF** status with me may not be the level of friendship for most, I truly feel so grateful to have so many really good friends that support me daily. Some of these people have come into my life from employment, some through gyms I have been at, and some friendships even started by simply following each other on social media. It's weird how the world works, isn't it?

I will say my tribe is so much more than my various friendship circles though. I am fortunate to have an amazing family, and I don't take that for granted. I've always known I hit the jackpot in that area, so I do attribute so much of my confidence to how I was raised.

If you feel encouraged as a child you grow up with a different sense of confidence, I am certain of that. You always have those people to fall back on. I grew up in a house with so much support and encouragement. My parents were at every game, every event, every art show, and not just my parents, but my aunts, uncles, and grandparents, too. I legit had my own cheerleading squad for pretty much everything I did, and that was tremendous in my growth as a person and belief in myself.

My parents did an incredible job raising me, and I have not said that nearly enough in my life. They allowed me to grow into the person I was and never tried to hold me back. As an adult doing dumb shit, they still supported and embraced me. Confidence comes from those around you, too. I liked weird things and always seemed to find my own weird path. I was extremely mouthy at times, yet I was incredibly introverted at others. I went through strange phases like everyone does, and never once did my parents try to halt me from being who I was. They let me make mistakes. They let me go through the weird phases. They instilled discipline and values and rules, but they also gave me the freedom to fail, succeed, and be Katie. It wasn't until I became an adult that I truly realized how critical that was to my confidence and own self-belief.

How I live my life can probably be annoying to some or a little extra to others, but my family has done nothing but allow me to be me 100% and have accepted me without question. I cuss a lot and always have (I blame my dad), and while my mom will sometimes roll her eyes at the F bombs being dropped, she knows this is just how I am. When I show up to a holiday wearing something over the top or fancier than the dress code, she doesn't think twice about it. The things I do, my "go big or go home" attitude, my constant desire to try new things that are scary to some….no one tries to cut me down. That goes for every member in my family, from my mom to my cousins to everyone in between. Family, thanks for being such dope ass human beings. You're the fucking best.

Why am I telling you this?

For starters, if you have a strong family base and friend circle **APPRECIATE IT**. I know for me personally I spent many years not realizing how fortunate I was to have these people in my life. It wasn't until I hit some incredibly rough patches and really started to evaluate my life that I was able to appreciate all those little moments and things I previously overlooked. I never realized how lucky I was to get to sit down and have a home cooked dinner every single night with my family until I realized I had friends who never ever had that luxury. The older we get the more we realize how important people and memories are, not material objects. I will forever miss Sunday dinners where my grandparents came over and we were just all together. Our holiday traditions…what I wouldn't give to be able to celebrate them how we used to before we lost some of our loved ones. I wish everyone could have some memories like that with their family that just make their heart happy and bring an instant smile to their face.

I never was big into gratitude when I was younger. In fact, you could say I found the thought of practicing it silly, yet the older I've gotten, the more I have realized its impact on my life. For the past five or so years, I have written in a gratitude journal every day. Sometimes the things I write are so simplistic, but other times they are deep and rock me to my core when I think about them.

I enjoy this time each day. I enjoy taking some time to **THINK** about the joy and the good that I have in my life every single day. It is a **CHOICE** to find it and to appreciate everything I am so fortunate to have instead of focusing on the things I do not have. I think so many of us focus on the latter because it is easy to say "I don't have this" or "I didn't do this", and often that takes over the good. I do think this has helped to contribute to me becoming a better version of myself, and my challenge to you is to start incorporating a gratitude practice in your life.

Maybe you don't want to journal, and that's ok. Maybe you just think about five things you were grateful for happening that day before you go to bed. Perhaps you write them down on pieces of paper and drop them into a jar to be read later. Maybe you download an app. Just find a way to bring gratitude and that positivity into your life. It does make a difference in the bigger picture, trust me on this.

What happens if you don't have a supportive family or your friendship circle is shit? I know there are those of you out there that this applies to, and you are reading this chapter rolling your eyes. Sometimes the most toxic people in our lives are blood relatives or people we have had in our lives for so long we question if we should end a friendship or relationship strictly based on time. It's time to switch gears to plants.... dead ones....

There's a strong possibility if you are in my circle you have heard me say this forty million times, but I am going to say this louder for the people in the back: **STOP WATERING DEAD PLANTS!** No, I'm not actually talking about plants. I can't keep any plant alive, so I sure as hell am not giving our gardening advice. I'm talking about **PEOPLE** and the relationships you keep!

Once you gain a strong sense of who you are or what you want in life and start vocalizing it, I think a few things rise to the surface really quickly. One of those: you see who is **REALLY** there for you. The other: you see who has fallen into the "dead plant" zone and needs to be weeded out.

I, unfortunately, have struggled with this big time as an adult, and even as I write this chapter my heart hurts a little bit at the fact I let some people get close to me who weren't truly there for me. For quite some time there I had dead plants in my life trying to disguise themselves, but luckily, I eventually saw them for what they were.

I never really considered the fact that I had dead plants in my circle until late 2015. My father had just unexpectedly died, and my life had changed overnight. From a personal perspective, I was reverting back to my early hot mess self: fighting urges to drink, negative self-talk, and unwarranted bouts of anger that had me wanting to fist fight everyone and everything. I was in a dark, dark place, as some of you who have gone through a traumatic loss may be able to relate to. I can tell you that I was not the best version of myself during that time, and I had discovered what the lowest of lows felt like. This time I didn't have my friend alcohol as my crutch to lean on like I had during rough patches in the past, and that make things a little bit rougher for not only me, but those around me.

As someone who had harnessed her inner Wonder Woman self and was living her best life right up to the loss of my dad, the one thing that was hardest for me to do was say "Hey, I need help." I didn't want to admit to anyone how bad I was struggling, and I was struggling a lot. I felt like Artax, the horse Atreyu was leading through the swamp in *The Neverending Story*…. slowly sinking and not getting ahead in any way.

Traumatic loss has this crazy way of making you feel like time is standing still while also flying by a million miles an hour. If you read that line and it doesn't make sense, that makes me happy because that means you haven't experienced a loss that has rocked your core like I am discussing. If you do get what I'm saying, my heart goes out to you. Grief is such a hard battle to fight daily. Sending you big hugs.

Since I had very few people in my life that had gone through something similar, I had to find my own way of talking about my grief. As many of us know, there are no rules with it; it impacts everyone differently and for many of us we struggle with the thought "is what we are feeling/thinking normal?" Part of me wanted to bottle things up inside and not talk about them; the other part needed to get what I was feeling out. I was so incredibly broken in so many ways, and I had no idea how I could **EVER** smile, laugh, or live again.

I made the decision from the beginning to share as much as I could about my journey with grief on my social media platforms and on my blog, and it is something I still do to this day. Writing about how I feel and the loss my family suffered helps keep the memory of my dad alive, and it also allows me to introduce him to those individuals who I met after we had lost him. It's important to me to have others know about that important part of my life, especially since I am a carbon copy of him. My mom always said I was my dad in a dress, and she was right. We were 100% two peas in a pod.

I do want to take this opportunity to say that it is very challenging dealing with someone who is grieving. I never realized it until I suffered the losses I did. After my dad died, two of my close friends each lost their fathers, and I saw grief completely differently since I now had been on both sides of it. It was hard to watch them struggle. It was hard to know how to best support them since their situations were so different. You want to be the best supportive friend you can be, but sometimes you feel like you are on eggshells. There are moments where everything you do or say feels like it is wrong, but you don't know how to navigate the situation. No one tells you this stuff growing up, and there is a reason for it: there is no instruction manual for this crazy thing called life, and sometimes you just have to figure it out as you go.

I know during the time of my dad's death many of my friends did not know how to deal with the situation or with me. I know I was a handful while also being fragile like a bomb that no one knew when (or if) I would explode with emotion or anger. Some were afraid to talk to me about it because they didn't want to upset me, and I understand. Still, they were there supporting me and just being there, even if no mention of my dad's death came up.

During those initial few months I remember just wanting to feel normal again. I wanted to feel alive again because so much of me felt dead inside. I wanted my friends to call me for coffee dates. I wanted them to tag me in silly weird posts on social media. I wanted to laugh again and be surrounded by the people who genuinely made my life better. Most of my squad did just that, and you will never know how much it meant to me. I don't know how I would've gotten through that time without those little pieces of normalcy.

There were a few close to me who showed their true colors during that time though, and man, did it hurt. One of the girls who I loved to run with and spend time with just oozed negativity every single time I spoke to her. I felt drained and exhausted, and I always felt bad about myself after interacting with her. She had a great way of making me feel that way, and even to this day, I am not sure why or how she became so unbelievably negative. I remember just wanting to get together and run because I needed that endorphin boost, but spending time with her never felt good. In my mind, I couldn't understand how someone who "cared" about me could try to kick me when I was down like I felt she consistently was doing.

Another girl who I had known for almost two decades followed closely in her footsteps, only taking on a self-centered route and getting angry at me for not being able to do things that served as emotional triggers for me. I remember sitting at my house wondering what I could do differently after explaining to her why I couldn't attend an event and how I was concerned I would ruin her good time if I did. I genuinely was concerned about being a buzzkill, and I know I was coming from a good place when I told her that. Instead of understanding, she attempted to berate me for it in the rudest possible way.

One thing that happened during the first few years battling grief: I became more cognizant of how my actions could affect other people. I don't think I was ever that self-aware in the past, and that was a huge area of growth for me. Even now looking back on some of those pivotal friendship moments, I am confident I handled them the best I could and in a way that was driven by love and genuine concern instead of a "woe is me" kind of attitude. I did my best in uncharted waters, and sometimes your best just has to be enough.

A huge lesson that I learned during that rough time: your mental health is more important than anything. It is more important than the money in your bank account, than your career, attending events, what other people think of you, what brand of purse you carry…...than **ANYTHING**. If taking care of yourself means you have to cut someone out of your life, cut them out. I cut both of those individuals out of my life, unfollowed them on social media, stopped any form of contact with them, and I haven't spoken to them since.   Have they crossed my mind a time or two? Absolutely.

It's challenging to break up with a friend, especially someone who has celebrated so many great life events with you and who has been in your life for such a long time, but sometimes that breakup is necessary for your mental and emotional wellbeing. As with the death of a loved one, you need to grieve for a friendship ending, too. I had to grieve the loss of those friendships because they had been such an important part of my life for so long, and it was hard to let them go, even with that being the best thing for me. As sad as it was, it was the best thing I could've done for myself mentally during such a rough time in my life, and I don't regret it one bit.

Dead plants don't just surface when you are going through loss like I did. That's just really when I truly became aware of their presence in my life, then I started to realize how many were floating around impacting other parts of my life. Know when they also tend to surface?

The correct answer: When things are going really well for you.

During the initial months of my weight loss journey, I found some people in my circle at that time really unsupportive. They did everything they could to sabotage me, like trying to bring in all kinds of unhealthy foods to the office to tempt me, teasing me in front of everyone, making comments about how I looked, even trying to strong arm me into drinking at office happy hours despite knowing I was working hard on my sobriety at the same time as my health. It hurt to be the butt of their jokes day in and day out, but I knew I couldn't let their words get to me. I didn't realize then that their motives were driven by their own unhappiness, but I do now.

That's the problem with the dead plants in your life: so many of them fall into that category because they are unhappy with themselves, their life, that they are jealous of something you are doing, etc, but instead of them focusing on themselves, they try to cut you down. In their world, this makes them feel better or gives them that distraction they need from addressing their own issues head on.

Even as I wrote this book, I dealt with some people who claimed to be "good friends" with me that actively tried to talk me out of publishing it and making snide comments. They were the same people who tried to make fun of me when I would get a tattoo I wanted or when I was cast to be in a workout program. When I mentioned wanting to move to the beach, they cut me down and told me all of the reasons I would hate it. They were the people in my life who were the happiest when they found out I was getting a divorce because it allowed them to attempt to pull me down to their own miserable level. It stemmed from jealousy and their own inability to get out of their comfort zones and chase down something they wanted in life.

If you have someone in your life acting that way and trying to cut down your choices, it is time you realize that is on **THEM** and not **YOU**. That dead plant needs to go because eventually it will bring you down, too. Pay attention to those who don't clap when you succeed. Those, my friend, are dead fucking plants in your life.

We have such a limited amount of time on this planet. I refuse to water down who I am for people who can't handle me or don't like me, and I refuse to give any of that time to people who truly are not adding value to my life. **PERIOD.** You shouldn't either.

There's a great quote out there (author unknown) that I think of **ALL THE DAMN TIME**. "Respect yourself enough to walk away from anything that no longer serves you, grows you, or makes you happy." People that do this to you are energy vampires, sucking the life and confidence out of you. Don't let the door hit you on the way out of my life. I will do anything and everything to protect my energy and the energy I bring to others, and I will not allow some piece of shit person to suck the good vibes and sparkle out of me. You should not let them do it to you either.

I know for many people the thought of cutting out a toxic family member can be heartbreaking. I will say if it comes down to the point where you **MUST** separate yourself from family, it will definitely be a little trickier than a friendship. There are so many avenues to take, but it has to start with communication. When it comes to the dead plants in my life, I started with trying to communicate how I was feeling to see if maybe their mindset was just different and if a conversation or ten could help us move forward. In the cases I mentioned, they didn't, and it was apparent quickly that things could not and would not improve. I went into the discussions I had establishing boundaries for myself and **MY PEACE OF MIND**, and when I knew that the goals I had for that relationship could not be met, I cut them out. I didn't make a hasty decision. I tried to find a resolution, but it didn't work.

The truth of the matter regarding dead plants: they've been holding dead weight in your life for way longer than that current moment. You've allowed them to stay past their welcome, and I would confidently say that you've probably known that for quite some time. I know I did. It is scary and sad to cut off ties with someone, and if you do it know you will go through the stages of grief like the loss of any relationship. Remember how we already committed to owning up to our bullshit? It applies here, too. Stop feeding yourself bullshit about the people impacting your life and happiness in a negative way. You deserve better.

Speaking of plants, focus on the good plants in your life. Reach out to those who are important to you and let them know how much you appreciate them. It could be exactly what they need to hear today.

Chapter 4
SELF-LOVE SCRIBBLES

Who are the good plants in your life?
What are you doing to "water" them today?

FIND THE SILVER LINING

Let's get into some heavy stuff here, ok? Heavy means the stuff that makes me cry and lets you into my soul a little more. I'm talking about rock bottom moments and how they can make and break us, especially when we don't have the confidence or belief in ourselves that we can overcome them.

If you are reading this and have never had a rock bottom moment, congratulations. I have had **TWO** thus far in my life, and they all have happened over a span of a few years. What a bag of laughs they have been! Just kidding….

Rock Bottom Moment #1: The first six months of 2013.

It's hard to pinpoint a specific moment where I went, "Holy shit, my life is a mess." Truth be told, there were so many moments I thought that. As we kicked off 2013, I was drinking heavily, which had been going on since probably about 2009-ish. Things really had kicked into overdrive with my bad habits that holiday season. As we have discussed, my relationship was a complete shitshow. I had found out he still had an active online dating profile and was dating other people secretly behind my back. When I confronted him about it, he would yell at me and call me names, which varied, but always involved some version of **FAT ASS**.

My eating habits were terrible. All fast food all the time. Supersize me pleasseeeeeeee, and the amount I was spending on my alcohol addiction was absurd. My clothes didn't fit, my self-esteem was in the shitter, I truly felt like I had nothing to offer, and I was scared to talk to anyone about it, which meant I was bottling up a whole bunch of stuff inside. I was at the lowest of the lows and felt completely hopeless. "This is just how my life is going to be" was the mentality I had.

Can anyone else relate to that? That feeling of just settling for a shitty life because there are some shitty things stacking up against you?

If we are being real here….I can't believe I got through that period in my life the way I did. I cringe thinking back to what I can remember from that time. I mentioned earlier about buying some fitness products when I was hammered, which aligned with one of my friends staging an intervention on me, and the impact those two things had on me. I can't even put into words how the timing of both of those events and just the events that happened after impacted me to keep me from plummeting even further. If days or weeks had happened between the two, I don't know if I would be where I am today with my health.

They say trust the timing of your life. I certainly do with how the star aligned for me during that time.

Then there's **Rock Bottom #2**: The death of my dad.

2015 was going to be my year. I was completely making it my bitch.

In September of 2015, I walked away from a 10 year+ career in higher education to officially be my own boss and run my own health and fitness coaching gig. I was ecstatic to help other women get connected to solutions to help them with their own goals and even more excited to help motivate them through their journey. I was excited to coach group fitness classes and get out of my comfort zone. This was my dream career, and I was **FINALLY** doing it.

On October 3, 2015 (Hello, *Mean Girls* day), I got married and was so over the moon happy. The wedding was everything I had hoped for and an amazing celebration with family and friends. "Man, things could not be better," I would say out loud. I was the healthiest and happiest I had ever been and felt on top of the world. Coming off the wedding high and getting into a groove with my own business, I just felt like I could tackle anything.

Then life was like……hold my beer. Or, in my case, hold my Shirley Temple.

November 20, 2015 started as most days did for me. Slowly with coffee, reading some personal development, and a little bit of hustle. The night before I had **FINALLY** wrapped up all the *Mad Men* episodes I had been binging and sat down to write a blog on Don Draper. After knocking that out, I needed to finalize some choreography for a dance class I was going to be teaching the next morning. It would be the largest class I had taught to that point in this format, and I was so excited and nervous that I wanted to make sure I nailed it.

As I danced around the living room I noticed my husband coming downstairs. Since his shift in the emergency room had ended just a few hours prior, I figured he was just grabbing a quick snack before going back to bed because this was a typical part of his routine. Instead of getting a snack, he headed toward me in the living room and said he wanted a hug. Since I am a hugger by nature, I thought nothing of it. He then asked me to sit on the couch.

I instantly felt like something was wrong, and my mind started to race with what he wanted to tell me. My mind immediately ran through about a hundred scenarios. Realistically, I was prepared for him to tell me my grandmother had passed away. She had just celebrated her 93rd birthday the week before and her health had been declining. I was not prepared for what he said next.

He told me my mom had just called him, and my father had died. **MY FATHER. MY MAIN SQUEEZE. MY ROLE MODEL. DEAD**. He was only 61 years old.

I sat there stunned, then remember throwing my phone across the room and screaming. Everything became a blur after that. I remember the time on the living room clock said 1:41pm. I remember calling my mom and screaming at her to stop lying to us. I truly thought she was making it up. My dad was the healthiest person I knew. He had just finished a six-mile run that morning. This has to be a mistake. That day, November 20th, 2015, my entire life changed. In addition, I, too, changed as a person.

I had always been one of those "things happen for a reason" people, and in a blink of an eye that mindset changed. There was no reason on this Earth that my dad needed taken from me at such a young age. **NONE.**

Over those next few weeks, I bounced back and forth between being my usually positive and upbeat self to a negative jerk. I spent a lot of time fighting the urge to drink. Up to that point, I had been sober for two years and three months, so some urges here and there, but zero slip ups. Losing my dad made me want to revert to my old ways and just drink myself into an oblivion so I could run from the pain.

But I didn't.

One thing that I had learned over the past two years of working on myself every day was that sometimes you have to run toward the pain, not away from it. I know that may sound crazy, but it is the truth. When I first shared publicly about my alcohol addiction, I was so terrified that I would be judged and talked about. I was still working on getting my confidence to the point where I could truly follow the FWTT mentality. I wanted to say "fuck what they think" but at that time I was more "fuck what some of them think." Sharing that on social media was beyond terrifying, but I focused on the fact that my mess could become my message, and I could share my personal triumphs to help inspire others. I kept thinking about the difference I could make in the lives of others with my story and what I had been able to overcome. That's still my thought process today.

So instead, I focused on two things: reflection and affirmations.

Each morning I would get up, make my coffee, and sit quietly for a few minutes before I read my personal development. I took that time to reflect on things I was grateful for from the day before. It gave me the opportunity to acknowledge the good in the day, because there is **ALWAYS** some good you can celebrate aka the silver lining. It was hard to find the good during those weeks following the death of my dad, but I would find it.... even the smallest thing. I remember one day the only thing good I could take away from that day was how delicious the mini pineapple upside cakes were from a bakery by my mom's house. That's how hard I had to search for the good at certain points. Shout out to Hogan's Bakery for making those cakes…10/10 recommend if you are ever in Columbiana County.

Then I read a list of affirmations that I have written down (also shared on the notepad on my phone for quick access) to remind myself of what I am capable of doing. The most important one I focused on: **I AM STRONG AGAINST NEGATIVE LIFE CIRCUMSTANCES AND REACT TO THEM POSITIVELY.**

This one is one of the most important affirmations then and still today. I still have it saved in the notepad on my phone. It stemmed from me thinking about a conversation with my dad where I was bitching about something (I can't even tell you what...but probably something miniscule), and he responded with "Life is 10% what happens to you and 90% how you react to it." I focused on that quote when my dad died. He sure did love that Charles Swindoll quote, but man, did it change the perspective for me.

The 10% in that situation: My father passed away unexpectedly. **I COULD NOT CHANGE THIS EVENT.** It had happened, and even though I cried and screamed and bartered with anyone who listened to bring him back to us, it was not going to happen.

The 90%: I could react in a way that could set me back in my life aka drink myself into an oblivion, complain about what had happened to me, play victim, revert back to bad eating and fitness habits, avoid showering and caring about my presentation, avoiding people, etc etc etc.

OR….

I could react in a way that would move me forward.

To me, this meant seeking help from a therapist, attending local Griefshare meetings, and focusing on my mental health each day by not drinking and by eating properly. It also meant me writing about this painful part of my life because I wanted to share my experience with others who were grieving to help them move forward positively, too. Most importantly, I just wanted to **DO GOOD** and make my dad proud, and I knew a sulky, drunk Katie would not do that. I made the choice to **BE STRONG AGAINST NEGATIVE CIRCUMSTANCES AND REACT TO THEM POSITIVELY**.

To this day, that is still a part of my morning routine. I wake up, I caffeinate, I reflect. I read my affirmations. I read whatever personal development book I am into at the time, and I write in my gratitude journal the things I am grateful for. Every night before bed, I reflect again, only on the good that happened that day. I cannot tell you how much it has helped my mindset.

Can I digress for a second and touch on the subject of personal development? When I first started my online health and wellness coaching biz, reading personal development for about fifteen minutes a day was something that was strongly encouraged. It was pretty much part of your daily job description. **I LAUGHED AT THIS LIKE A FREAKING HYENA**. I don't need to read any of those "self-help" books I would scoff. Here we are years later and I have written one. How ironic. BRB, going to go fire up some Alanis Morissette

I don't know why we as a culture have made it seem like reading any kind of self-help book is bad. The term itself has such a negative connotation. I clearly agreed based on my initial response when told I needed some PD in my life. You want to know what made me jump on the bandwagon of PD? *The Shawshank Redemption*. Yep, the movie! If you know me on a personal level, you know I loooveeeeee movies. *Shawshank* is one of my absolute favorites. One day I was watching it for the gazillionth time, and good ol' Andy Dufresne dropped one of his best lines in the movie. "Get busy living or get busy dying." I don't know why that day I really focused on it, but I did, and I started to think about growth.

I've always heard the line that if you aren't growing you are dying, and somehow Andy's quote that day made me think about what I was and **WASN'T** doing to grow as a person. I decided I would give personal development a try. Check it out, all the hours I devoted to movie watching paid off!

But **FIRST**…. I had to get a little real with myself. All growth comes from that place, so if you are reading this saying to yourself "I don't know what I need to work on," go pour yourself a cup of coffee, grab a pen if you don't have one handy, and let's get real with ourselves. Okkkurrrttttttttt?

What do I mean when I say get real with ourselves? We need to identify the areas we suck at the most. Remember owning up to our bullshit? This is tied directly to that. Are you someone who wants to be a leader, but struggles with leading anything, even your dog back in from the yard? Are you a perfectionist with the "I'm never good enough" mentality? Do you feel stuck or unhappy? Make a list and, honey, that list better be kind of long. **NONE** of us are perfect, and we all have areas of growth. If your list has only one or two things, own up to your bullshit. You have more to work on than what you are writing, so be honest with yourself so you can work to become your best self.

What do we do once we get our list made? We seek out personal development books that cover that topic.

When I got real with myself, I knew one of the biggest things I struggled with was this little thing called **PATIENCE**. Sound familiar? I wanted success overnight with my business, and I would get pissed when it took longer than I "thought' it should take. That acknowledgment made me realize that not only did I suck at patience, but I straight sucked at running my own business. I had no clue what it all took, and I was like a lost puppy dog wandering around. The first few book choices I read focused on those topics. I took everything I could out of those pages and my mind became a sponge. I wanted to be better. I needed to be better. Personal development helped me with that.

Moral of the story: You have to embrace the suck to become a better (fill in the blank with your goal here). Maybe you are reading this scratching your head because you aren't an entrepreneur like me. That's totally fine. You may just want to work on being a better spouse or parent or friend. There are books on everything! Just identify where you suck and go from there.

I do get asked all the time what books I would suggest to someone looking for new personal development books. I love so many that it is difficult to answer this question, especially depending on what area of life you want to improve, but there are a few authors that have my attention with everything they write. Again, I cannot stress enough the importance of seeking out books based on areas where you are struggling. I've got recommendations on books if you are looking to get sober, the importance of being single, forming habits, just looking for an easy read….you name it. I could write a book on book recommendations…I have that many!

 If you are in the market for some new reading material, my favorites include:

Anything by Gary Vaynerchuk.

His social media is one I stalk daily, and after getting to hear him speak at a conference, I was all up in the Gary Vee sauce. Know why I love him so much? He had embraced the FWTT thought process before it was even a thing and truly does not give a flying **FUCK** what anyone has to say about him. I admire his boldness and his straightforward approach. Beyond that, **WOW,** what a badass entrepreneur he is.

Anything by Grant Cardone.

The 10x Rule is one of my top books of all time because it just fires me up to do more and push myself to not be mediocre. I'm all about leveling up, and from a business perspective that man challenges me. His books just push me to give me absolute best.

Anything by Mel Robbins.

Oh, Mel. You changed my life with *The 5 Second Rule* mentality, and I am just obsessed. Robbins is one of the first people/things I think about when I wake up every morning because of this concept. Yes, I still have to apply that rule daily. We aren't always motivated, friends! Beyond that, I just really appreciate her approach to life. You can find me stalking her social media daily, too.

Anything by Jen Sincero.

Here's a fun fact: Jen Sincero was the **SECOND** person on the planet who knew what the title of this book was going to be, second only to my mother. Shortly after I determined the name, I went to an event where Jen was speaking, and I got to talk to her after. I told her I was working on my first book, and when she asked me the name I hesitated, then I was like "It's Jen Fucking Sincero. She needs to know." I told her, and I promised to mail her a copy when it came out. I still have the picture of us in this moment on my phone. Jen is someone who, like Gary Vee, is straightforward and just a **BOSS** at telling it like it is. I just love her and her writing, and I basically think she, Mel Robbins, and myself should be best friends. I'm putting it out there, guys, let's become literary besties. Time to get a group text going.

Honestly guys, there are **SO MANY** great books out there. If you aren't into reading, no biggie. Find an audio book or podcast…. just something to help you grow! You just have to seek out growth material that will work for improving the areas of suck in your life. Put your pride aside, make the list, and start attacking it. Personal Development is the secret sauce….in growth, in success, in being a good ass person.

One little thought on identifying your shortcomings and working toward them: doing that allows you to take back power of your life because you are identifying **YOUR** suck and are working on correcting yourself as opposed to blaming others. Let that sink in. When you stop blaming, start accepting, and start actively working to get past something, you're growing. You are becoming more confident, and you are working toward that best version of you.

Some of you guys know I played college basketball, and while I loved the sport, I had a very challenging relationship with both the college Athletic Director and the basketball coach, which forced us to have some heated discussions. The AD was the kind of person who was completely full of himself and would constantly try to talk down to you to make you feel like you were nothing. That kind of person **DOES NOT JIVE WITH ME.** Pair someone like that with a basketball coach who was even worse with manipulation, gaslighting, using a condescending tone 24/7, and just a complete hothead, and you've got a recipe for disaster.

I loved basketball, but the collegiate level is different. Part of me wasn't completely sold on playing a sport in college, but the athlete in me could never imagine not. Since I was torn, I made the decision to go to a D3 school in the event I decided to stop playing at any point. I didn't want to lose any scholarship money, and at a D3 school there were no athletic scholarships, so everything I had earned was considered academic. It was a strategy to get the best of both worlds, financial assistance and the chance to see if I liked college ball without the threat of losing everything if it wasn't my cup of tea.

It wasn't. I'm a coffee lover, and I didn't like tea at all.

Pretty soon into my first season, I knew I wasn't vibing with the collegiate basketball experience. Everything revolved around the sport, and I didn't like it one bit. If I wasn't in class, I was at practice, lifting, running, study tables, or some other predetermined activity. My love for the sport was fading, and that wasn't a good feeling. What used to be so much fun and exciting for me had become a burden and a chore that I dreaded, and I didn't know what to do.

Because of my major, I had some classes that conflicted big time with practices, and my coach consistently would approach me to try to switch my major to something else that would "fit practice times better". It got so bad that when I would be able to go home on the weekends to see my family, I would cry the entire drive back to campus and get so worked up I would legit puke. I dreaded going to practice and being a part of the team. The love for the game and enjoyment I had for it had been stolen.

That was a point where I really needed to have a sit down, drag out fight with myself. What did I want to do? At this point I knew I did not want to return to the team for the following season, but I was worried about letting down my family and my team. I still hadn't adopted the FWTT mentality, clearly. Some other things were happening around that time with the team, including me getting written up for getting drunk and rowdy in the dorms while playing Tetris, and everything led to a meeting with my parents and the AD. Our coach wanted to label me as a troublemaker on the team and was set on punishing those of us involved as much as she could.

I remember very little from that conversation because I was just not into it, but I do remember him telling me specifically to, "Katie, point the thumb, not the finger." When I had shared about how poorly myself and the members of our team were being treated, he didn't want to hear it. To him, we were the problem, not the coach or the unethical things going on behind the scenes. I remember leaving there so angry at him trying to tell me all of this was my fault. It's also when I **REALLY** learned what gaslighting was about.

As I do, I wanted **SOME** good to come from the situation and the meeting. I took that line he said to me and made a mental note of it, and I apply it to my life now all the time. I add that here because sometimes you really need to look at that driving force as to why you feel the way you do, why the problems are happening around you, what you can control, etc. Is it a situation where you should be pointing the finger? Or the thumb? If it's the thumb, then you know where to head in terms of personal development books, podcasts, etc.

Back to Rock Bottoms……because sometimes I go off on tangents, and that's ok. I do what I want.

JK Rowling once said, "Rock Bottom became the solid foundation on which I rebuilt my life." Friends, I don't think a quote ever touched me more in my entire life. Why? Because my life….my success….my happiness….it all came from rock bottom moments. The rough moments where I thought I was down and out without a chance of redemption became a springboard to better, bigger, and happier moments for me. Look at what JK did with **HER** rock bottom. Good things can happen from them, and she is proof. So am I.

My daily thought during my rock bottom days: how was I going to survive this? I had no choice. I had to find a way.

Every single one of us is going to be faced with some rough AF stuff over the course of our lives. I don't say that to be negative; I say that because it is a part of life. We have to deal with losses, unexpected changes, and rock bottom moments. They are scary, unpredictable, awful, and are full of moments where you wonder if you'll be able to make it through.

The question is: when you hit those moments….the moments where you truly wonder if you are going to be able to move on and ever get back to a place of happiness again….will you choose to put up a fight or will you give in and wallow????

90% of life is how you react to it. I'm not saying it is going to be easy. I'm saying you have to acknowledge the shitstorm you are in and **MAKE THE FUCKING CHOICE** to take back control of your life and fight for that happiness.

Your choice to go after the good is the reaction you want.

Your choice to not let some nasty chapter in life take everything else from you is the reaction you want.

Your choice to **RISE UP ALWAYS** is the reaction you want.

Your choice to open the fucking umbrella and **WALK INTO THAT STORM** like fucking boss. That's your storm, and you are going to own it.

Remember, it's ok to get knocked down. No life is complete without a fair share of moments where we think we are down and out. You've just got to want to get back up when they happen.

"And once the storm is over, you won't remember how you made it through, how you managed to survive. You may not even be sure, whether the storm is really over. But one thing is certain. When you come out of the storm, you won't be the same person who walked in." -Haruki Murakami

Chapter 5
SELF-LOVE SCRIBBLES

What are areas in my life where I can grow?

EMBRACE AN ALTER EGO

I know, I know….an alter ego?

What are we, Clark Kent? Or five years old?

All jokes aside, this girl **ONE MILLION PERCENT** believes you need to have some kind of badass alter ego to help power you through the bullshit, especially when you are in the beginning stages of a confidence makeover. Ever hear that "fake it til you make it" line? Yeah, sometimes you have to embrace that. I sure did!

Back in the low confidence days aka that time in my life where I cared about what people thought and genuinely made life choices based on what I thought they would want me to do, I remember sitting on my couch watching these women on tv who seemed confident AF with who they were and I was like…...How. Does. One. Get. To. Be. This. Way? So, as most normal people would do, I decided to pretend a bit.

I sat there and thought about **WHO** was a strong woman that I loved and admired and someone who I wanted to be just like. One woman was at the top of the list: my ongoing obsession, Wonder Woman. I've always been connected to her since I was a little girl, and I don't care if she is fictional or not, a Wonder Woman mindset is what I wanted to have so a Wonder Woman mindset was what I was going to fake.

Think about WW for a minute. She was fearless. She had self-belief even when others tried to talk her out of doing things. As a child, she dulled her sparkle by hiding those superpowers we all have come to know she possesses. She was unbelievably strong and curious and, above all, demonstrated compassion towards others. We can also throw in the fact that she is somewhat stubborn, opinionated, and competitive. Sound like me? My mother is currently shaking her head in agreement.

Ok, so I know who I admire, Katie, now what? If you don't have someone in mind, think about who you love and admire and **WHY** they came to mind. Feel free to jot the reasons down in your notebook or on the worksheet in the back of this chapter to reference later if needed. I did a total brain dump of everything I knew and loved about WW. Physical traits. Personality traits. Core Values. **EVERYTHING**. You may think something is miniscule or too small to jot down, but do it anyway. All of those characteristics are important to acknowledge and see on paper as you think about who **YOU** are and what you want to improve.

The next step is you making an action plan and putting into practice the things you admire about that person. You don't have to have the go big or go home mentality. Start small with one or two things. For me, the first thing I started working on was my self-belief. I dove into personal development and podcasts and started to step outside of my comfort zone as we previously discussed.

You know what I was most nervous about back then? Using social media as a platform to influence others. **I WAS TERRIFIED!**

After losing close to seventy pounds, I finally mustered up the courage to post that before and after. I was terrified and so scared of what others would say (again, we go back to that thought process). I had one "friend" private message me asking me to take my pics down. He said they bothered him because he thought they were gross. I definitely didn't take those pics down, but I definitely did utilize my right to hit the **DEFRIEND** button.

And then there were the internet trolls. Guys, can I just tell you that **I STILL DEAL WITH THEM TODAY**. They are everywhere, and we will be talking more about them later in this book. I got accused of photoshopping my pics (not that talented, sorry). I was told I looked like a whale before and after (hey, go fuck off), and I had a lot of people just have some kind of opinion on how I was living my life and what I was sharing about it. People just feel so much power being a keyboard warrior and talking smack from behind a screen, don't they? That is one sure sign that they need to get working on loving themselves and improving their own confidence, because they are projecting their own insecurities on others, which is not okay.

The more I stepped out of my comfort zone on a consistent basis, the easier it got. That's the thing about working on yourself. If you do it a little each day, it eventually becomes a habit, and in turn you become more comfortable with it. Confidence is a muscle you must work every day. I repeat, you must work on it every single day!

My alter ego developed fully after a long day at the office over a decade ago. It was one of those days where your coffee needs coffee and everyone has figured out a way to get on your last nerve. We know those days, right? I was literally holding in rage all day because of some different things that had compounded, and I thought I was doing a really great job keeping my cool. One of my coworkers made a joke. "Looks like Hurricane Katie is about to hit. Take cover!" It wasn't far from the truth.

I'm one of those people that I am really chill and mellow 98% of the time. However, I go from 1-10 incredibly fast when I get mad or upset, and it shows. My neck gets all red and blotchy and my eyes make it clear to get out of my way. Nothing could describe me better than a Hurricane, thus Hurri-Kate was born.

That name had come to my coworker's mind not just because of my attitude that day, but because of the chaos I brought when I would drink. We haven't talked about that a ton thus far, but friends, let's talk for a second to talk about good ol' drinking Katie.

Now that I am actively approaching my tenth year of sobriety, I find so many conversations stemming from people about my journey with this, especially conversations with new connections. My decision to live a sober life was definitely one that had some help in the beginning, but ultimately, it was my choice to continue it, and it has been the best decision I could have ever made. Sure, without alcohol, I've gotten into shape, lost the weight I gained from all that Kahlua, saved a shit ton of money because y'all…. alcohol really adds up…. yadda yadda. But the biggest glow up being sober did for me? I regained control of **MYSELF** and my inner Hurri-Kate.

Too many of you were familiar with Katie in the bar scene (those of you who partied with me while I lived in Pittsburgh know it all too well) and saw first-hand the chaos she would cause. No, it's not just about how loud I would get when drunk (yes, louder than normal, which is hard to believe) or the excessive amount of high fives I would give, it was my overall asshole behavior. I literally would pick fights with everyone…. guys, girls, it didn't matter. I'd throw drinks on people, they'd throw them back, run my mouth, brawls would happen….it was **NEVER** pretty. I got thrown out of way too many places to mention and was just a sloppy mess. Basically, I was writing checks my ass could not cash…. or wasn't sure if I could cash. Fortunately, I never managed to get into any major trouble other than getting banned from the gym I went to at the time. To this day, I am not sure how I was able to escape without getting into any major trouble, but I am thankful I didn't and definitely don't recommend that behavior to anyone.

Friends, I did not like that person. I did not like who I was when drinking. I am cringing right now thinking about what a mess and sad, angry, and bitter person I was back then. I did not like the position I would put my friends in when I would be getting into drunk fights. 10/10 would not recommend being around me during that period of my life. I was also a dead plant to so many people; I brought nothing but negativity and trouble. Yes, I got cut out of people's lives because of my behavior. Yes, it hurt, but yes, it was warranted. I do not blame them one bit for cutting ties with me because my behavior gave them no choice.

The time Hurri-Kate was born was such a messy time of my life. I noticed something when I was in that Hurri-Kate state though. I didn't hold back what I wanted/needed to say. I didn't care what people thought of me. I stood up for myself. Even though it may have been a terrifying state for some and fueled by alcohol, I truly was at my most honest, best self at that moment because I was being honest and speaking my mind (not picking fights, let's clarify that now).

I wasn't being a doormat. It was that boldness, fearlessness, and strong will of Wonder Woman coming out. It took a long time to accept that there was good from that time period in my life. There's always **SOME** kind of good. You just have to be willing to see it.

A while back I took an Enneagram personality test just to see what it would say about me and if it was accurate. I scored a Type Eight: The Challenger. "Challengers are direct, self-reliant, self-confident, and protective." Yep, me 100%. Other qualities of an Eight include a fiery passion, stubbornness, a fierce look, independent AF, energetic, headstrong, and intimidating. Again, those who know me are shaking their heads in agreement. All of those definitely describe me.

If you haven't taken an Enneagram test, I highly recommend adding it to your To Do list. There are tons of free ones on the internet, and they help you learn about yourself, as well as identify areas of weakness. On the flip, they help you learn more about others, and, especially in relationships, they help you learn how to coexist and communicate better with others and their personalities. This also can help as you are working through that bullshit we already discussed and identifying weaker areas you can focus on for PD and growth.

As I was reading through all of the traits associated with my Enneagram type, it took me back to that couch day when I thought about those I admire. So many of those characteristics are Wonder Woman-esque. Those characteristics were things that I have always had; I just had to work on bringing them out. It took Hurri-Kate to make me realize that.

Really, Hurri-Kate is now just an extension of who I am. It's who I always was, but a person I watered down for so long. Having that alter ego in the beginning helped me find the courage to find my voice and really embrace who I was, even if it sounds silly to some.

Your alter ego represents everything you want to be. Confident AF? Yes, please. Bold and unapologetically you? Yep. Assertive and unafraid to go after what you want in life? You bet!

You know why you need to have that alter ego? To pump you up and throw yourself the pep rally you sometimes need to have. We know when those pep rally moments are needed…. like when you get dressed for work and look in the mirror and think, "Gosh, I look (insert variety of negative adjectives here)." Words are powerful, and the more negative ones you tell yourself the more apt you are to believe them. It's like a mantra, but a bad one you don't need! Adopting the mindset of that alter ego can help.

Little bit of homework for you: What are the things you want your alter ego to possess? Write them down.

Who are the people you admire, not just famous celebrities, but people in your everyday world? Write them down, too. What do you admire about them? Be as clear and concise and descriptive as you possibly can with this. The more info you dump here, the better.

WRITE IT ALL! Do a brain dump while listening to a song that you love, and if you don't have that one killer song that gets you going and feeling good, add making a bomb ass feel good playlist to your to do list. You need one.

Chapter 6
SELF-LOVE SCRIBBLES

What are the things you want your alter ego to possess?

Chapter 6
SELF-LOVE SCRIBBLES

Who are people you admire and what do you admire about them?

DITCH THE ATTITUDE

Confidence is something that you don't work hard to achieve and **BOOM**…. it's there to stay. As I have already said, it is a muscle and has to be worked every single day. If I say that enough over the course of this book, it will forever be imprinted on your brain, right?!

Let me let you in on a little secret. Negativity in your life will absolutely challenge your confidence, which is tied directly to your mindset, and if you allow it, it will tear down everything you have worked so hard to build. That's why I focus so much on that growth aspect and constantly working to be the best version of you.

Of all the lessons I have learned over the past decade, tapping into that mindset is one of the absolute most important lessons. I never realized how much simple thoughts and word choices could steamroll someone and just come for their confidence in such an aggressive way.

This happened to me.

TWICE.

Because apparently one time isn't enough for me.

I guess I've always just been an overachiever.

The first time I felt my confidence was being challenged was right after my father passed away. There I was, a shell of a human being, who was basically just sitting around my mom's house in a somber state spewing negativity, which is not like me at all. I was easily traveling through the stages of grief but was very caught up in the anger stage for longer than I probably should've been. Why was my dad taken from us? Why wasn't it someone else? I would think about some of the absolutely awful human beings walking the Earth and didn't understand why they weren't taken but such an incredibly good person was. That was a super popular thought I had almost daily for quite some time. I was angry, and that anger transferred into bitterness, which all helped fuel the huge ball of negative energy I was living in at that time.

My negativity was compounding at a rapid pace.

One of my all-time favorite personal development lessons is centered around the thought of how thoughts, actions, feelings, etc. build up over time. Think of a snowball as it is coming down a snowy mountain. It's growing with every spin on its way down, picking up momentum and getting larger and larger by the second. Before you know it, that snowball is too big to stop and is a powerful force. Negative thoughts and actions can quickly become that snowball if we aren't careful. If you haven't read *The Compound Effect* by Darren Hardy, do yourself a favor and add it to your shopping cart this very second.

During that time of my life, the tail end of 2015, I was living in the most negative way. Every little negative thought and statement was building up inside of me. I was having a hard time posting on social media during that time because I almost felt fraudulent. In my mind, I was less than inspiring. How could I inspire anyone while being such a negative asshole? How could I do my job? I would look in the mirror and see a snarl on my face instead of my usual smile or RBF (it's a chronic condition...I can't help that I was born with a strong resting bitch face) and think **WHO IS THIS PERSON?** I was starting to not like what I said, how I felt or how I acted, and there was a brief time where I just wanted to give up and quit everything.

Yes, friends, your girl said the **Q** word.

Deep down, I truly thought I should quit my health and fitness coaching business because I just had nothing to offer. Part of me wanted to quit working out because why be healthy? My dad was robbed from a long life, and he was the healthiest person I have ever met, from his nutrition to his exercise routine, and look what had happened. Every single thing in my life had me wanting to just quit and become a recluse.

Shortly after that thought came into my mind, I was going through a bunch of papers and found a print out of something my dad had given me long before. It was a page of quotes he had typed out after one of our arguments where he had scribbled some notes by each. I'm sure you have noticed by now that I love quotes, and my dad did as well. For some reason, I just needed to see his handwriting that day, and finding that was absolutely what I needed in that moment. I also found something else that was instrumental in me getting my shit together. It was a poem I had written during an English class in college titled *I will Rise*.

I remember sitting there reading this poem, which was simple with the focus of rising from the ashes. I had written it just after the 9/11 attacks and had meant for it to be a poem about us as a country rising above the attacks and hate, yet it hit me differently reading it all these years later. I sat there thinking about how it applied to me at this point and how I had to rise above this thing that had happened to me. Yes, I was buried in the ashes at that particular moment. I had been to hell and back with no warning, and I was still deep in the fiery parts of hell where my spirit was broken.

But……

There was also a girl down there with a warrior spirit, one that had always risen above, and one that now, more than ever, needed to rise. From that day on when I woke in the morning, I would look in the mirror and say out loud, "Today I will Rise." Some days I would throw an F bomb in there if I was feeling particularly spicy, but I always said it. It came to be a reminder of the confident person I had become….of my Hurri-Kate self...and it also reminded me I was not a victim of my circumstances. In fact, that statement…. that whole "I will Rise" mentality means so much to me it is tattooed on my left wrist, a spot I can see all day every single day to make sure I never forget that I can rise above anything that comes my way.

I'm going to go off on a tangent here because I need to, and it involves one of my pet peeves.

PET PEEVE: People who let their circumstances dictate their future.

I 100% believe that **YOU, yes YOU, READING THIS**, have the power to overcome anything that has happened in your past. It's going to require a confidence makeover, a mindset shift, a lot of hard work, and the ability to own up to your bullshit, but you can overcome anything if deep down you really want to.

Someone out there will definitely try to challenge me on this, but I will stand firm as fuck on it. Bad shit happens to everyone, sometimes all at the same time, and sometimes without an explanation. It **HAPPENED TO US**. It does not determine our future unless we allow it to. Remember the quote my dad told me: life is 10% what happens to you and 90% how you react to it. You must decide to not let the shitty circumstances that happened to you **DEFINE** who you are as a person is a decision you must make to move forward in life. Bottom line.

I look at my circumstances and cringe when I think what I could've been like if I let them consume me. Most people know I lost my dad because I talk about it so frequently, but what you don't know is that the year before I lost my dad unexpectedly, I also lost my aunt suddenly and a very dear friend as a result of a horrible car crash. Ten months after losing my dad, I lost my grandmother, the sole remaining member of my dad's side of the family. The year following, I lost my maternal grandmother following a long battle with Alzheimer's. In a very short timeframe, I lost some of the most important people in my life, not to mention the fact that my marriage was ending. It was one loss after another, and I had **EVERY** reason to be bitter and continue on that way.

I had a choice. I had a choice to be a sucky person and live that " I am a victim life" or **DO SOMETHING** positive with it.

My choice was to work hard to educate others on grief and my experience with it. My choice was to be a good fucking person and do everything I could to help others however I could. My choice was to live a life that had all of the loved ones I had lost smiling down with pride. I made the choice that day after I found that poem to dust myself off and rise like the motherfucking warrior I am. You have a choice, too. You are not defined by what happened to you unless you choose to. And **YES**, regardless of what it is, how horrible it is, or how challenging life may seem, **YOU ALWAYS HAVE A CHOICE.**

Hoping off that soapbox now…. getting back to the confidence being challenged thing….

My confidence was challenged again when it was apparent my marriage was over, and I needed to move on. I won't go into details of that because they really have no place in this book, but I will tell you that it was a blow to my {strong} ego when we made the decision to go separate ways. That **Q** word I mentioned before…. I felt like I was definitely quitting on a person when that wasn't the case, and that was a hard pill for me to swallow.

There was a period where I reverted back to that negative part of me **AGAIN** and would call my mom crying and just saying awful things about myself to her. I remember at one point she broke out her stern mom voice (we know they all have one) and said, "**KATIE ELIZABETH**. You are the most positive and inspiring person I know. Why are you not practicing what you preach?" I thought about that, and she was right. Moms usually are.

I know for many people a divorce/dissolution situation can be a very nasty thing, and for those of you who have to go through that, my heart goes out to you. It is a difficult thing regardless, but I can't imagine how challenging it is when your life feels like a warzone. I feel very fortunate that going through the process we did not have any animosity or nastiness, and that we were able to get through it like mature adults with respect for each other. That isn't to say there weren't tough moments and tough days, because there absolutely were. To this day, my ex and I are still close, and I feel very lucky to have him as a friend, ally, co-dog parent, and supporter in my life even if we are no longer partners.

If we are being honest, which we are here always, I attribute that to my self-growth as a human being and constantly working on being a good person who knows her worth (ties right back into confidence). The old me...that sad soul slinging back White Russians…was also petty AF. Like the death of my dad, the death of this relationship was one that had happened, and I had the choice to move forward in a way that was good for me and my health or in a negative way. I opted to see the good in the situation. Instead of be petty and trivial about things, I chose to be supportive and kind. Things may not have worked out as I had thought they would, but instead of being bitter, I became better, and I am thankful for that.

When I was in the deep end of that time frame, I immersed myself in positivity. Affirmations, personal development books, podcasts, and Netflix specials like Brene Brown's *The Call to*

Courage helped me more than I could ever put into words. I really focused on spending time with those in my life who made me level up and be a better person. Have you ever heard that you are the sum of the five people you spend the most time with? There's truth in that. I spent time with individuals who were positive and uplifting and badass girlbosses who reminded me that I was a warrior and would be okay. I can tell you that choosing to eliminate those dead plants I previously mentioned did me so much good, especially at this time in my life.

It was interesting how many people felt the need to send me messages or comment on my social media posts with surprise when it came out that I was no longer married. There were some people who wanted to press for details, people who actually made comments that they felt they were entitled to know what was going on in my life since I share so much on social media, and some people that just wanted to try to be gossipy and get some tea.

That's not how I jive, friends.

Some people couldn't believe I didn't talk about it openly in posts. Did I need to? Absolutely not. I had zero interest in sharing any elements of our separation with the public, and there was absolutely no way I was going to sit around running my mouth in a negative fashion about the situation either. To me, that says more about **YOU** than anything else. I had/have nothing negative to say about my ex and am happy we are in the place we are where he doesn't get pissed if I slap the big head filter on him on Tik Tok and where we can send each other funny memes that only we get why we are sending them.

How you handle a shitty situation speaks volumes to who you are as a person. Remember that when you want to get nasty. It's all about respect. Respect for others, respect for yourself, and respect for your situation.

As I mentioned earlier, you have to look for the good in every single situation, which means finding that silver lining. Even the shittiest of the shitty situations can have something good in it. Acknowledging the good things does not mean you are glad the bad thing happened. It just means you are **DOING YOUR BEST** with the cards you have been given.

My dad's loss did bring good into my life, but it is because I allowed it to happen. It doesn't make me miss him any less, and I still would do anything to have him here with us. My eyes opened so much after we lost him, and I was able to appreciate my family and friends more. I have been able to help many other grieving individuals on their grief journey, and I have been able to impact some people who needed the inspiration and positivity, as well as trying to educate others on what it is like to deal with a traumatizing loss like I did. There's good in that.

Let's make a promise, ok?

No more "Woe is me."

Instead, how about a little "Woooooo is me" (done in your best Ric Flair voice) and the belief that regardless of what is thrown at us, we will end up on top.

Chapter 7

SELF-LOVE SCRIBBLES

What are some silver linings you can find from rough patches you have experienced in your life?

UNPACK YOUR BAGGAGE

There are days when I think back to the way I used to be, back when I lacked confidence and really depended on the validation of others to feel good about myself, and I am shocked that I lived so much of my life that way. If you are in the thick of a confidence reboot right now, you may not be able to relate to that statement, but my hope is that someday soon you will be able to. My hope is also that you'll be able to look back on the way you were before you figured out you are a bomb ass human and say, "**WOW**, look how much I've grown," or "My life is so much better now because of x, y, and z."

Have you ever taken some time for some solid reflection on who you were? I refused to do it for the longest time. I refused to do a lot of things, which you may have noticed. I guess you could say I have a little bit of stubbornness in my veins along with the glitter. I realized this when I immersed myself in that whole "owning up to my bullshit" thing. Reflection is **HARD**, y'all. Getting real with yourself is never easy. No one ever really wants to say "Hey, I really sucked as a person because of (fill in the blank), but it is a must to grow and evolve as a human being.

In the beginning of my health transformation, I was challenged by an online coach to spend fifteen minutes every Sunday reflecting on the previous week. I would reflect on how my nutrition was, how my workouts went, how I felt, and just how I was feeling about life that week overall. At first, I thought it was **S-T-U-P-I-D.** I just didn't want to spend time evaluating all of the things I was doing wrong that week because… **HONESTY ALERT**… I was at about a 75% fuck up level for those beginning few months. I made lots of mistakes, I constantly felt like I was failing, and I just did not understand the point of reviewing those errors. All of those fuckups were part of my very extensive baggage collection.

Let's talk about baggage for a second. Friends, we all have it. I am constantly reminding us of that because there are some people out there who will straight up **REFUSE** to admit it, but we all do. Every last one of us. And most of us, **ME ESPECIALLY BACK THEN**, try to bury it and ignore its presence.

Emotional baggage is definitely a weird thing, and I'm not sure how I developed the skills I did to compartmentalize it and bury it as well as I did. I pretended it wasn't a thing for a really long time, and I would call it "my switch" because, like a light switch, I could turn my emotions off quickly like it was nothing. Definitely not healthy, that's for sure, but I think the root of that was just not wanting to truly process what I was dealing with or admitting to others with the fear they may see me as a failure or train wreck even though I was.

Getting back into the reflection discussion…..

When I finally decided to jump into these fifteen minutes of reflection every Sunday, I started to unpack that baggage faster than I wanted to. Reflection for me was almost a rabbit hole, and I fell down it quicker than cruising through Tik Tok for a few laughs. You already know how that goes. One video turns into ten turns into an hour. Before you know it, **OMG** where did the day go? That kind of rabbit hole. I'd realize I only stopped at

McDonald's twice that week instead of eight times, so that was a win, but also an opportunity. I got my workouts in…. yay for me! I increased my water intake, and I went to bed twenty minutes earlier. It always was easy to reflect on those black and white areas with my health and fitness journey because they were so easy to track and identify.

There was the one part of reflection that I would save until the end, and that, my friends, was when the baggage showed itself. How was I feeling about life that week? And where was I at when it came to happiness?

UGH.
CRINGE.
VOMIT.

Reflection made me face the one thing I already knew: I wasn't happy. But why? With so many things seemingly going in the right direction, why was I not happy?

During my reflection one week, I decided to just do a brain dump of all the things that I wanted to work on to improve my happiness level. I think initially I thought it would be a small handful of things, but before you knew it an entire sheet of paper front and back had been filled. I may have had an emotional meltdown with a pint of Ben and Jerry's directly following that.

I do want to caution those that read this that reflection is kind of like a soul cleansing emotional—am-I-on-my-period-because-I-am-so-hormonal--all over the place kind of thing. **AS IT SHOULD BE.** So, if you are reading this and want to work on yourself through reflection, I highly encourage you to a) have tissues handy b) spend time by yourself doing this or with a pet because they won't judge you c) have your comfort snacks handy. Reese's PB cups never let me down. Neither did Cheddar and Sour Cream chips. Clearly donuts are always a star in my life, too.

After the reflection brain dump, I made a solid decision to work on one thing every single week that was on that piece of paper. I ranked them, from easiest to hardest. **WHY?** I am all about the small wins. I **STILL** tell my clients to go after the small wins every single day. They add up and end up being a big win eventually. Plus, those small wins build up confidence. If you are someone who is struggling with that confidence piece (which I'm guessing you are or you wouldn't be reading this book), you've got to build confidence where you can. **START SMALL**.

Your baggage and your bullshit very much are a tag team effort. As you are making the list of all the bullshit you are feeding yourself, keep that list handy for when you start to really unpack that baggage. Have the two lists side by side. Brace yourself though: that baggage could be one specific event or a series of events, and sometimes it takes a while to emotionally go through them.

I do want to say, therapy is a **SOLID** choice. Never, ever, ever be ashamed if you feel so overwhelmed by the things going on in your life and that are challenging your confidence to seek out professional help. It used to be so taboo to talk about going to a therapist, but nowadays I feel like everyone has (or should have) one on speed dial.

As I mentioned in the disclaimer of this book, I clearly am not a professional. I simply am sharing what worked/works for me. However, sometimes your baggage may be so incredibly deep you truly need time with a professional to sort it out. It is also extremely beneficial to have someone neutral in your life to offer their insight to what is happening. We all love our family and friends, but we know they are biased sometimes with their opinion of what we should do, who we should be with, how we should cope with something, etc.

I've sought out professional help many times throughout the course of my life, and I am not ashamed of that one bit. Believe it or not, my parents had me go when I was younger. The driving force: I was a smart mouth asshole for a brief period and was always getting into fights with my dad, making for a less than desirable home environment for my mother and brother. It's so hard for me to fathom there was a time we would be at each other's throats because once I became an adult we had such an awesome friendship and relationship, but believe it or not, I was a hothead back in the day. I had to get in the last word, I was snarky, and I was just a mess. Seeing a professional helped back then. I also made the decision to seek out help again after my dad passed away.

Honestly, my decision to go once we lost my dad wasn't that I needed to unpack any baggage. That's the thing with confidence, reflection and doing some of the things I have already mentioned: the more you do them, the more confident you become, yes, but you also become more **SELF-AWARE.** I was very self-aware with my feelings and the stages of grief I was going through. I didn't need any help unpacking any of that.

What I did need was someone to just listen to me vent and bitch, so I went to a therapist and did just that. I think it is important when making the decision to go to a professional that you walk in with a goal of what you want to accomplish. With anything in life, if you don't know what you want to achieve, how will you ever do it?

I needed to verbally get out all of the things I was feeling, and I wanted to do it in a space where I did not feel anyone else's bias would enter the discussion. I knew if I didn't, it would weigh on me in a major way, and I did not want to bottle up my feelings or emotional distress. I had to confront those things head on so I could make progress in my own grief journey.

I know every single human being is different, and we all carry different baggage. For some people, it may take a lifetime to unpack it. It is scary to address it, it is scary to work through it, and for many people, it is scary to let some of that go. However, your growth, your happiness, and your success are all being hindered by negative baggage weighing you down. I know it was so much for me.

We are living in an age where so many people are talking about mental health, and I am so thankful for it. For so long, society seemed to look down on people who struggled with it. I'm thankful now there are so many resources to help when someone is struggling. And friends…. this is your reminder we all struggle.

Please do not be afraid to talk to someone and seek out whatever help you may need. Mental health has to be a top priority **ALWAYS.**

Chapter 8

SELF-LOVE SCRIBBLES

What are areas in my life where I would like to be happier?

Review that list and rank them easiest to hardest to fix.

IGNORE THE KEYBOARD WARRIORS

I absolutely cannot and will not avoid the topic of haters, trolls, and gremlins, especially when it comes to anything confidence related. Can anyone kill your confidence more than those things? I think not.

Has anyone else ever felt so insecure that you chose to tear down others because you allowed your own insecurity to take over?

Guilty as charged.

The old me used to do that all the time. Why? It didn't make me feel better. I **KNOW** every single person reading this has done it at some point. Think of that *Mean Girls* scene where everyone closes their eyes and raises their hands if they have had a girl say something bad about them behind their back or if they have said something bad about someone else. If I asked you to raise your hand right now, you would. We are all raising our hands.

Nowadays, with social media being the thing that everyone's doing, we've gotten to see a new warrior tribe surface, and they are the worst kind of warriors on the planet. Those, my friends, are the keyboard warriors. You know the type: people who sit behind their computer screens and just comment shitty comments or send nastygrams into your DM for no reason other than they are miserable with their own lives and spewing hate makes them feel good.

Let me tell you, I've been dealing with these gremlins now for almost an entire decade as I've run my online business through social media. I've had awful, awful things said to me by people who I don't even know who they are and who know nothing about me. The first couple times I experienced this I truly did not know how to react. I remember sitting there looking at the comment/DM thinking "**WTF** did I do to get such an ignorant rude comment?"

If you know me, you know I am no scaredy-cat of confrontation. In fact, I actually really love a solid confrontation because I know that there will be some kind of end result. To me, there is nothing worse than an argument or misunderstanding that doesn't have a resolution. Know if we ever get into an argument or disagreement, I'm coming for you to confront you because I want to squash it and move on, either harmoniously or just going our separate ways. Confrontation can be very healthy when done right. It is how adults handle things.

Back to those trolls.

It is really difficult to confront some asshat you don't know who is just bored trying to start shit, because let's face it: that's what the majority of those people do. I think the old me could easily be classified as somewhat of a loose cannon who needed to think before she would speak. That got me in trouble…. **A LOT**. It was just my nature to bite back right away, so in that first year of working through social media, any time a troll would come for me or slide into my DMs, I flipped a bitch switch and went right back after them. For some reason, my gut instinct was "attack them back". I got into some pretty heated arguments that I'm not proud of back then. I guess you could say I was being kind of trollish myself. Whatever it is, it was not a quality I liked in myself. Definitely baggage I had to unpack.

My baggage: feeling like I needed to defend myself. Back then, I would get so wrapped up in other people's opinions because I just wasn't confident in who I was, and I was insecure about the things that they were targeting. Since I lacked confidence and couldn't really pull the FWTT card at that time, I would just try to hit them below the belt a little lower than they hit me. Tit for Tat, right?

I realized whenever this would happen that it felt good while in the moment to strike back, but it did not feel good after the fact. I always hated how I felt and wanted to hash it out and make it okay, but sometimes words are so damaging you know there is no going back after you threw fire. There were times I would hit that **SEND** button and instantly have regret for what I said and how I said it. I should've listened to my mother more when she would say, "Think before you speak." I definitely didn't in those hothead days.

Let's fast forward to today. I still deal with gremlins. A lot of them. Groundbreaking newsflash: they will never ever go away. Someone will always be down on themselves, insecure with who they are, and trying to pick fights, which is sad, but true. If you are reading this thinking there is some magic plan of action to rid them from your life, unless you live in a bubble and remove yourself 100% from society, that won't happen.

People will message me and say I'm too skinny…. or I'm too fat…. or that I shouldn't dress the way I do for my age. I have people attack me all the time for choosing to eat donuts when I am a health and fitness coach. I have people accuse me of subscribing to "diet culture". I'm too over the top. I'm too basic. My tattoos are stupid. I should tone down my cussing. I'm not a good role model for young ladies. I'm not authentic because of this or that or who knows what. I hear it all. It's always from people who I couldn't pick out from a line up because they are people who I have **NO CLUE** who they are. Gotta love those people. If you are that consumed in following what I am doing though, I probably wouldn't call you a hater, but more of a fan. Just sayin'.

Moving on……

What can you do? Focus on what **YOU** do….aka how you **REACT**.

Yes, I'm going back to that quote my Dad etched in my brain again, but it is just such a classic quote that is just straight fire that needs to be sad again and again.

Here's what I did with the trolls then, and even now what I do.

I PAUSE.

A great lesson I have learned as time has gone on is how important it is to practice the pause. What does this mean? Take time to let something really sink in. Take time to let something marinate. Just take time without being rash or crazy. Just freaking pause.

I think for many people (I know I am guilty as charged at this), we are so crazy busy and in that go-go-go mentality that we always are rushing to the next thing, the next appointment, the next (fill in the blank here). We are so busy being crazy that we forget to pause and enjoy life. We also forget to pause and focus, think, and simmer down when we get heated. It's just the way society is right now. We rush everything and lack patience.

A troll comments on something of mine on social or sends me a DM…what should I do? Instead of that instant reaction, I stop and pause, then I think to myself, "Is this person worth having a discussion with?" 9.9 times out of 10 the answer is a huge **NO**.

If they are someone who I value in my life, then I know I need to respond, and that response is usually coming by way of a face to face discussion or phone call. It's not going to be a petty DM or reply to a comment on social media.

Are trolls valuable?

ABSOLUTELY NOT, sis. They are weird little toys you used to collect and store on a shelf when you were little. They have no place in your life or in your head, so they deserve zero fucks, zero energy, and zero space in your mind. Why do you let them rent space in your mind when they have no business being there??!!! Fucking evict them to make space for the good people and the good energy!

Once you've identified the person as having no value in your life, move the heck on. Delete the comment, unfollow the person, block them…. whatever you need to do. Here's the beauty of living in a social media driven world: You are not obligated to follow, comment, or socialize with anyone you **DO NOT WANT TO**. I'm at a point in my life that if you try some of that garbage with me, I just cut you out right then and there. I've never utilized the block feature so much in my life, and boy, do I love it. Byeeeeeeeeeeee.

Here's the other thing you need to realize: **NOT EVERYONE DESERVES ACCESS TO YOU**. If it comes down to it and the troll activity is high, flip your shit to private and **DON'T** give them access. Just because many people share every single aspect of their life on social media, does not mean you have to. Just because you once shared everything, doesn't mean you **STILL** have to. Only **YOU** know who deserves access to the elements of your life you want to share.

Initially, working a business through social media had me feeling some type of way, like I had to share all the things. When it comes to my life, there are always things that I refuse to get into great detail about, like relationships. So much of what I do is public, and that is okay. I want to inspire you with my workouts, triumphs, and struggles. What I don't want to do though is be disrespectful or discuss private matters. Sometimes that's hard for others to get, especially those trolls only coming to your page/stories for a big glass of whatever tea they think you are serving.

I'll tell you the exact moment when I realized how obnoxious and annoying trolls were. No, it wasn't when they would call me fat or nasty or any of that body shaming hogwash that initially flooded my DMs. It was one day when I casually mentioned in my post something about divorce (literally said the word and no details), and a follower slid into my DMs faster than a kid on a Slip 'N Slide in 100+ degree weather. She asked when I posted about the divorce because she couldn't believe she missed it and wanted to go check it out. When I told her I didn't because…. **I DIDN'T** (also a long ass time had passed at the point…like **LONG ASS TIME**), she said, "But I follow you, I'm entitled to know what's going on."

Currently rolling my eyes recounting this memory.

Homegirl actually used the term **ENTITLED** like me having a public social media account gave her free reign of every aspect of my life. My face in that moment could clearly be used as the picture in the dictionary next to **"WTF"** because I could not believe the audacity of this woman. Who says this?

I'd like to insert here that Homegirl also was someone who very frequently would bash the MLM I am associated with on her page and also had accused me of being "brainwashed." MmmmmKay. She also was a person I had **NEVER** met **ONCE** in real life. I could tell you not one personal detail about her, and other than what she saw on social media, could not tell you one detail about me.

This woman kept going on a rant trying to throw blows at me that I was fake and lacked authenticity because I didn't share with my audience the details of my divorce. I ended up just blocking her, and I really hope by now she has grown up a little.

The one thing she said that really irritated me…. **LIKE REALLY IRRITATED**...was that I was not authentic because I did not share details of my divorce (technically dissolution if we are being specific).

YO, HOLD UP. The one thing I pride myself on and have always been proud of is my authenticity. What you see on social media is me, good and bad. If you've ever watched my stories, you know I share the good stuff, the inspirational stuff, the rants, and spend time on my soap box often. There are days I'm glammed up, and there are days that I look like I was rolling around in a muddy field without a hairbrush for days. I am who I am in whatever moment I surface on social media, and I do that because I never ever want to meet someone who follows me and then have them walk away totally confused on who I am as a person. That's just not my vibe. I'm multifaceted, but I take pride in being a real, authentic human being.

I share this because early on in my business days, I ended up in an elevator with one of the top coaches in my industry, and I was so excited to meet her. I had followed her on social media and just thought she was incredible. While in that elevator, I saw a whole different side to her. She was **NOTHING** like she portrayed on social media and was so rude to me that I walked out of that elevator completely questioning so many people in my newsfeed and industry. I knew then I could never ever feel good about being that way and promised myself in that moment to never try to be anything I wasn't. I think about that moment often.

What you see is what you get with me. If you don't like it, move along. That's okay with me, I swear! As my girl Jasmine Starr says, "Everything you do should attract and repel others." We shouldn't all appeal to everyone. There will be some people who don't like us and the way we are, the clothes we wear, the word choices we make, and we will, in turn, repel them. Again, that's okay, sis!

I know many of you run businesses through social media, and I just wanted to remind you how important it is to just always be your best, most authentic self. It's exhausting to be anything **BUT YOURSELF**. Know this though: you can be authentic without spilling the items in your life that are truly private. That's called having respect. That's called having boundaries. I respect my ex-husband and our situation and have zero interest in just sharing details that are not relevant just so you have something else to read while you are on the toilet.

Before the internet though.... yes, believe it or not, some of us lived that life.... the trolls and haters walked among us, and we received the shade face to face. You may still be dealing with them in this capacity, because as I mentioned, trolls never really ever go away. They can be found in all shapes and sizes, all age ranges, all genders, all parts of the world.

We discussed dead plants, but I truly believe those people (aka "the plants") at one point meant something to you in your life. They played a part in your life story, and you valued them. Trolls and haters are a little different. Even though a once trusted person can turn into one, trolls and haters are typically people who know very little about you or have very little meaning in your life. Sometimes these people may not be downright malicious like some trolls can be, yet they still bring that presence and negativity to your life, cut you down, and make you question your worth.

I remember the first time someone told me I couldn't do something and made me question my worth. I should clarify: the first time someone told me I couldn't do something, and I made the decision to prove them wrong and work on my confidence, even though it was basically nonexistent.

I was in seventh grade, a gangly and awkward girl rocking Sally Jessy Raphael-esque red glasses that had been given the name "Birdlegs" because of my toothpick like legs and skinny frame. My goal: to play on our junior high basketball team.

As someone who attended a very small school system in Northeast Ohio, we didn't have to deal with the issues of larger schools, like having to go through "cuts" to be on the team. If you wanted to participate in a sport, you pretty much could. My father was a stellar basketball player, and I had hopes of being one, too, so once basketball season rolled around, I showed up with the other girls in my grade eager to start playing.

It was obvious that of all the girls at practice, I was one of the worst. At that age, I lacked confidence and skill, and it appeared as if I had zero athletic ability, which caused me to land a seat on the bench with the other third stringers. After a few practices, our coach pulled me aside and asked how I was doing and also what my goals were with basketball. Contrary to my poor performance, I was having a lot of fun learning the sport and practicing, and I shared this with him, as well as my goal of playing varsity someday. I wanted to be just like my dad.

At that moment, I saw our coach, a younger guy who hadn't been out of college for too long, chuckle under his breath. He said something that I still remember clear as day: "You'll never play varsity. You should try a different sport. This isn't the sport for you." He said it with such confidence, and I truly believed him in that moment.

As he walked away from me, I stood there in my usual awkward gazelle-like stance fighting back tears. My friends hadn't heard what he had said, and I didn't want them to see me cry. How embarrassing! I thought about going to the pay phone to call my parents to come get me, but since practice was nearly over, I finished it out.

When I got home, I went into my room and had an existential meltdown, the meltdown I was too embarrassed to have after my coach crushed my dreams. My father heard me and came into my room, naturally asking what was wrong. I told him, and without even hesitating he said, "If you want to play varsity, we are going to make it happen." I didn't know how, but I believed him.

I finished out that season riding the pine as a third stringer, getting very little court time and improving very little. Since it was winter and Ohio winters are wretched and unpredictable, my only time working on my skills was during practice, and that was minimal. My heart was still set on playing varsity and improving my skills, so I stayed focused by watching NBA games and learning as much as could. I had to watch every game my favorite player, Scottie Pippen, was playing in, and I would get so excited about the next time I would be on the court.

Once summer hit, my dad started working with me. Every night, I would go outside to our basketball hoop and shoot free throw after free throw. Once I completed those, I would move on to layups, then dribbling exercises, then jump shots. I did this every night all summer long. My dad would join me most nights, helping me with my form and encouraging me. On days he worked late, I would still practice. "Don't forget about your goals," he would say, and I wouldn't. There were days I didn't want to practice, there were days I would cry about it, resulting into huge arguments, but I kept practicing. My dad said it would pay off, and I believed him.

Was he right? You better believe it.

I graduated in June of 1999, wrapping up an amazing high school athletic career. My senior year was everything my seventh-grade self hoped for and more. My team had advanced on to win Districts, the first time in our school history the women had earned this title, and I not only played varsity, but served as one of the captains of our basketball team with my best friend, Kelly. My personal accomplishments included being named Player of the Year and earning me multiple unanimous first team selections, including First Team All Ohio.

In my final game on our home court, I shattered the single game scoring record of forty-two by scoring fifty-seven points in a single game, a record that still stands at my school and has me ranked at number fourteen in the Ohio High School Athletic Association record books as of the day this is published. I was heavily recruited and went on to play college basketball, later getting inducted into my high school's Hall of Fame.

When I think back on that time period now, I don't look so much at the accolades or the records, but rather at me disproving someone who felt the need to tell me I wasn't capable of doing something. Did it hurt to be told I couldn't do something? Absolutely. Did it fuel a fire in me to be the best I could be? You better believe it. It was easily one of the most pivotal moments of my life.

I think about that moment often and how drastically that could have altered the course of my life had I listened to that coach. I can pretty much guarantee you have had something similar happen to you during the course of your life. Maybe it wasn't a basketball coach who made you feel like you couldn't do something. Maybe it was a parent, or a friend, or maybe even your spouse. We all have people in our life that are those energy vampires, people who are sucking the positivity and dreams away from us a little at a time. In fact, sometimes these people become a broken record, saying the same negative thoughts over and over, causing us to actually believe the nonsense they are saying.

As I've gotten older, I've realized how critical it is to believe in yourself and the internal power you have that can get you through anything, regardless of what life throws at you, but it's not easy, my friends.

That day my little seventh grade self had her heart broken about her varsity basketball dreams, and that wasn't the last time I was told I couldn't. That was only the beginning. I now keep the basketball from the night I hit for fifty-seven in my office to remind me every day that I won't let others tell me what I can or can't do. I'll decide that for myself, thank you very much.

The sooner you learn to love who you are and what you have to offer the world, the easier it is to let the troll hate roll off your back like it's nothing. Because, sis….it truly is nothing. There will always be someone against you and someone who challenges your worth.

Just don't ever let it be you.

Chapter 9

SELF-LOVE SCRIBBLES

When has someone told you that you **COULDN'T** do something and you believed them?

BE A KID AGAIN.
REALLY.

DO NOT read that chapter title and think "this does not apply to me." I don't care how mature you think you are, how old you are, or how distinguished you think you are. Deep down inside of each and every one of us is a childlike spirit begging to come out. **DO NOT** keep that spirit buried!

I wanted to touch on this because it is something over the past few years I have really tried to focus on, and while childlike as an adjective may come across in some kind of way, it really boils down to this: simple joy.

I think back to when I was a young kid (I'm talking pre-junior high age here) and how happy I was during that time. So many simple things brought me joy back then like getting a new book, riding my bike to Roose's drug store with a dollar and buying a ton of candy from their candy wall, and eating ice cream with my friends at the local ice cream shop after our softball games.

Isn't it crazy how the smallest things back then brought us so much happiness? Can we all just commit right now to approaching life with the same enthusiasm and excitement as we did as a five or six year old child?

Where are you at with joy in your life right now? As in today, this very minute as you read this? Does it have a presence in your life? If you think about it too long then you know your answer….it doesn't.

As we get older, those small joys tend to disappear, but only if we let them. I noticed in my own life I became overcome with stress, fear, insecurity, and doubts. Let's not forget dealing with the adult duties of having to work and pay bills, dealing with heartaches, getting passed over for promotions at work, and all of the things that can rob you of joy. Back when I did that reflection exercise I shared with you regarding my happiness, this became so apparent to me. I had nothing bringing me joy like when I was a child.

I lost joy in my adult life for longer than I care to admit. Ironically, it was during the time when my confidence and self-esteem were in the dumpster. Joy ties into confidence because surrounding ourselves with things we love boosts our overall happiness. If we are happier and more positive, it is so much easier for us to gain confidence or maintain it.

I sat down one day and started thinking about all the things I loved that I didn't do anymore or make time for, and honestly, while looking at the list I was shocked at **HOW MANY** I no longer made a priority in my life. Even things like writing, something I used to do all the time, had been pushed to the back burner.

Reflection, as we have talked about already, is such an important piece of growth, and I want to reiterate that it can be done and should be done on any and every aspect of your life and **OFTEN**. I'm telling you that again because you need to think about joy in your life…. what brings it to you and where it is missing in your life. Again, go deep with this because sometimes we mislabel what brings us joy. I know I did.

I "thought" getting blackout drunk brought me joy for a long time. I looked forward to it and I enjoyed it in the moment, so I was happy right? That was a joyful time of day? No….no it wasn't.

I subscribe to the theory of fake joy **ONE MILLION PERCENT,** meaning things that appear to bring us joy, but they are just masking something else instead. That's what alcohol did for me. Often it may seem difficult to identify what is bringing us joy and what is bringing us joy in the fake sense. We get tricked because of emotions or circumstances, and more times than not we are telling ourselves we like something or it makes us happy because our partner or those in our lives love it.

I remember back to my drinking days when I was at the worst of the worst with my self-esteem and still involved with that on-again off-again mindfuck of a relationship that consumed too much of my life. Not only did I like to think that alcohol made me happy, but I also got to thinking and believing being a recluse did, too. He was someone who never wanted to be out in the social scene, with zero interest in going to sporting events, taking hikes, going to parties, going out to eat, etc. His idea of a good time and being happy was sitting on the couch drinking every single night every single weekend. Since it made him happy, I started to tell myself that it brought me joy, too. "It's nice to sit on the couch and drink together," I would tell myself.

Don't get me wrong, I love nights in on the couch and cuddling and movies and murder documentaries, but I have so many other interests and what makes me happy than that. Back in that time frame, drinking and tv watching were the **ONLY** two things I was doing outside of work. I am not exaggerating here…. I literally did **NOTHING** else. If you know me, you know I am extroverted and active, so these behaviors and the lack of joy and happiness in life were much more apparent to those on the outside of my life looking in than I was able to see.

Around the time of everything crumbling and me diving into reflection and personal growth, I read somewhere about making a joy list or happiness list. The article I found suggested just sitting down and doing a huge brain dump sharing everything that made you happy. It did not matter how large or how small the thing was. If it brought you even the teensy tiniest form of joy, it was going on the list.

Real talk time. In the beginning it was hard to write down an extensive list. I had probably the most generic list ever that included my family, friends, donuts, and my dog. Of course, those things made (and still make) me happy, but the point of the list is to really get back to the basics of those little things that bring us joy.

If I decided to make a list right now, I would probably have to set a timer, otherwise I'd be here for longer than I probably should, and my whole day would be thrown off. Why? I'm appreciating so much more these days. I'm choosing to see that good. I'm choosing to smile and be happy.

That list would include the beautiful donut I ate this morning, the new playlist I created with some killer workout tunes, the conversation I had with my brother, the fact that I woke up to a clean house because I actually cleaned my kitchen before bed, listening to my pug snoring, a text from a friend, starting to read a brand new book, getting to coach members of our fitness community at the gym, walking on the beach without shoes on, the recipe I tried that was incredible, the time I took for myself to meditate peacefully this morning, and the new somewhat trashy tv show I started binging. All little things that made me happy and feel good.

The goal of making a list and getting back to those childlike moments of joy is to take action and **START MAKING THEM A PRIORITY**. I look at my lists (because trust me…. I make them constantly), and I look at how I can incorporate them more into my day. At one point my list had "take a social media break" because it made me happy to detach from some of the toxicity that was floating around the innerwebs. After reading it on my list, I made a conscientious effort every day to take a break. It made me happier and feel better.

Make time for the things that make you happy. It may only take a second or two to enjoy them or do them, but that can build up and be magical with your mood and attitude.

So what are you waiting for…. go make that list and be a kid again.

STAT!

Chapter 10
SELF-LOVE SCRIBBLES

What in your life brings you joy?

LOVE EVERY VERSION OF YOURSELF

Have you ever thought about how many versions of yourself there have been and will be? We are constantly evolving, and that is one of the most beautiful things in life. I am not the same Katie today as I was yesterday. The Katie tomorrow... she will be different than today. Every day we are growing, evolving, and becoming better versions of ourselves. Well, that should be the goal.

Change is hard, and when I look back at my own personal evolution, I realized that the choices I was making were making others uncomfortable. That's what was making it hard for me. I was still (for a short time) caring about what other people thought about me. Let's take a second to go back to chapter one: **FUCK WHAT THEY THINK.**

Ok, now we are doing that…. **MOVING ON.**

Evolution of oneself means those around you are going to be forced to a) realize they are living a stagnant life and not going outside of their comfort zone and/or b) need to **LEVEL THE HELL UP.** People trying to talk you out of doing something/chasing a dream/making a change/just doing **SOMETHING**? Chances are they are trying to bring you down so you can **STAY DOWN** with them because they don't want to do anything more or challenge themselves. It is easy to be complacent. That's why so many people do it. My favorite thing people who are complacent do: they try to remind you that this or that didn't work, what happened back with so and so, etc. People who are complacent are constantly trying to live in the past and keep you there with them.

This happened a lot with me, especially when I made the decision to sober up and get away from alcohol. As I mentioned, those beginning months….even that first year: **HARD AF**. I was constantly at battle with myself and my mind to stay on track. I was constantly tempted. I was still dealing with shame of how my life had gone to get me to that point. And, on top of it, there were some people who really wanted to point out all those things.

Why? They missed their drinking buddy. They missed the person who would always go to happy hour and would always grab the tab. They missed the person they could make fun of or laugh at when I was at that blackout drunk level being a complete asshole. My choices and that version of myself made them feel better for their own choices. It gave them peace of mind because they weren't alone and someone else was making the bad choices with them.

I think about that version of Katie every single day. She struggled, she wanted to give up so many times, she was scared but determined. That version of Katie gave today's version **EVERYTHING**. I fought like hell during that time for a better life, for better health, and I made it happen. **THAT** version of me helped me develop the fight I needed. I'm thankful every day she did not give up and fought to be better.

I appreciate every version of myself that I have been, even that gangly little birdlegs version that lacked confidence that was told she could never play varsity basketball. Who we are today is a constant reminder or who we have been, what we have overcome, and how we have grown. It also makes us appreciate ourselves more. I am grateful for the confidence I have now, for the inner warrior attitude that makes me **ME**. I am grateful for my wit, for my loud mouth, and for my bluntness. Sure, sometimes all these parts of me still bring some chaos, but they are parts of me that couldn't and wouldn't exist without those previous versions doing the work.

When I look back to the old me….who the **FUCK** was that person?

SERIOUSLY.

So much of who I was two decades ago….one decade ago…. was a watered down, less than stellar version of myself. I think a big part of that was I got comfortable being comfortable. We've all been there, and don't even try to bullshit me or yourself and act like you haven't. We get into a groove, a rhythm, and we feel safe, so we just hover in that place with no forward or backward motion. This could be with relationships, jobs, workouts routines, where we live, friendships…. literally everything in life.

Why are we settling? Is that fun? It wasn't to me. There were so many times that I thought about how I needed to move on and get out of that comfort zone, but…. I just didn't. I know for me I was just scared. For me at that point, staying the same was easier than going into the unknown. I was scared of failing. I was scared of not being happy. I was scared of being worse off.

Fear is a huge thing that is associated with confidence and growth because it holds us back. It is the one thing in our mind we tell ourselves is okay to give into because we are scared. We listen to that voice and just keep on keepin' on in the same mundane pattern of life we have been doing. It's easier to just do that then attack that fear head on, right?

Don't get me wrong: I have some things I am fearful of that I am always working toward. We all do. How do we get past that? Fire up that list, sis. As we know, list making forces you to get real with yourself. When you put the pen to paper and just brain dump those fears and insecurities then you can start **TAKING ACTION**. If you are someone who is visual, like me, having things written down just brings them to life. At least it does for me **EVERY SINGLE TIME**.

The first time I did this I was shocked at what I wrote down. So many of my fears were things that now I look back at and wonder **WTF** was going through my head.

Some of these included:

-Being afraid people would call me names
-Being afraid people would make fun of me or unfollow me
-Being afraid people wouldn't want to date me
-Being afraid my family would be ashamed of me
-Being afraid I would get weird looks
-Being afraid I wouldn't be included in things

-Being afraid I would be judged or stereotyped
-Being afraid people would talk about me behind my back
-Heights
-Frogs
-Octopus (I know, it is weird, but they creep me TF out)

Ignoring the heights thing (that's a real thing, y'all) and the octopus/frog thing.... those other fears had **NOTHING TO DO WITH ME!** They were focused on other people! Go ahead and revisit that first chapter and repeat after me: **FUCK WHAT THEY THINK.**

Have you seriously started to notice **HOW MUCH** goes back to others? It's no wonder so many people struggle with this and struggle with their own confidence because we are surrounded by people, by social media, by magazines, by **EVERYTHING** trying to tell us how to think/act/look/be. We are fearful because so much of society **WANTS** us to be.

Fear stunts growth potential, especially when it is at the hands of others. If I am afraid of something, let it be for no other reason than **ME** holding myself back. There's no way in hell I will be fearful of what someone else may think. Heights? That's on me. No one made me afraid of standing on the top of a ladder, it's just something that has always scared me. Me being afraid of **YOU** not liking the way I answer a question or what I wear to a certain party…. that has nothing to do with me and is on you if you don't like my outfit or choice of words.

I truly believe fear holds us back from sometimes embracing the versions of ourselves that aren't so great. We will **NEVER** be an awesome freaking person every single day, that just isn't how life works. Thanks to social media and people constantly posting how "great" their life is (thanks, highlight reel only people...you know who you are), we may think it is not acceptable or okay to be that not-so-great version. Because of that, we hide it.

We are scared to show those true colors. We are scared to show our messy home, our screaming kids, our makeup-less faces. When we have meltdowns and cry and are having an awful day, it's easier to not share about it than to worry about someone judging us for our behavior, look, reaction, etc.

I touch on this topic many times in this book, but I cannot stress enough how important it is to just **BE.**

BE YOUR DAMN SELF, good and bad, beautiful and ugly, happy and sad…. all the versions of you!

I really forced myself to sit down at one point and think about the impact social media has on others (and their self-esteem), and I came to the realization that I had a gift. We **ALL** have a gift. We all have a story. I realized that the things I had gone through and my own personal evolution as a person could help more people and make more of an impact if I was just **ME**. Good ol' Katie, not some watered-down version that doesn't cuss as much or hides her constant RBF.

So what if my posts and opinions and stories pissed off people or annoyed them? So what if they unfollowed me? So what if they didn't want to be my friend any longer in real life? I didn't care. I knew my story and journey could inspire and help so many others.

To me, inspiring ten people to be their best selves or to believe in themselves or just go after that thing they always wanted to do was wayyyyy better than having 10,000 followers who just creep on my shit with no purpose.

It's been a minute, so let's take a moment to reflect and make another list. While you may be thinking, "Katie, I'm sick of list making," know these simple tasks help you grow, evolve, and reflect, not just now, but over time. This is something you can constantly add to or review, especially when you may be walking into a season of self-doubt.

I want you to write down all of the times you felt awesome, badass, beautiful, strong, confident, etc. Times that stick out in your memory as versions of you that were just **INCREDIBLE**.

I think about when I hit that scoring record in high school, a sorority formal in college, when I was elected to help our National Council choose a new President, getting an email from a client hitting a significant goal in her journey, how I felt in my pink wedding dress, finishing my first half marathon, a vacation with my family, when I was cast in a workout program, a trip I was on with friends. There are certain outfits that come to mind that I just felt great in. Celebrations, weddings, leadership events....so many! Even simple times like having coffee with my dad on our deck bullshitting. Write out as many as you can, just a good old-fashioned brain dump of those moments where you felt invincible or just amazing.

Once you have all of those written down, flip the script. Take a moment to brain dump all of the moments where you felt your absolute **WORST.** I'm talking about moments you did not think you were ever going to survive, where you questioned everything, where living seemed hard and crying was the only choice. As we have touched on already, brain dumping this stuff could get emotionally charged. Emotions are ok. Let them out as they surface and recognize them as part of your growth.

Losing my dad was at the top of that list, but I also think about when my parents' neighbors poisoned and killed my pug, Simon. I think about a break up that completely broke me in ways I've never been broken. I think about waking up in a bush after passing out drunk in it one night in college. There were promotions I didn't get at work, personal goals I missed achieving, getting rejected for various things or by people. Thinking about some of those moments right now makes me cringe. Those were all times where I was a less than stellar version of myself.

Why do this exercise?

All of those moments…. all of those cringeworthy **UGH I WISH THAT DIDN'T HAPPEN** moments contributed to who you are today. They contributed to the version of who you are, they contributed to the areas of your life where you lack confidence or are searching for growth in. So much of becoming a confident person who loves who they are is understanding all of the pieces that got you to that point, and even though some of those moments are rough, there is good and a silver lining in every single one of them.

Once you've got those lists done, a little reverse engineering needs to happen. It's basically a dissection of that moment to get to the root of the issue and determining what you can do with that to be a better version of yourself for tomorrow's version of you. I'm a huge fan of reverse engineering and really breaking things down for the naked eye to see. All too often we just see something at the surface level, but we don't dive deep into it to really determine how we got there, why things happened as they did, or what we can take from them in a positive way.

Take the incident I mentioned above where my pug was poisoned by my parents' neighbors at the time. I won't go into all of the details of it, but I will say it was an absolutely awful situation that did **NOT** have to happen. At that time, the version of myself that surfaced was one of the ugliest versions of myself I have ever seen. I was full of hate. I wanted revenge. I seriously contemplated many, many acts of revenge that are unspeakable. My hate and disgust for those people led to me avoiding visiting my parents' house for months after because I did **NOT** trust myself and my actions. Yes, this was also during my drinking days, so I was completely a loose cannon. Every single time I would pull in my parents' driveway I wondered if that would be the day I would go off on them, because trust me, I wanted to in the worst way.

I went through so many emotions with the loss of Simon, who was my first pug and first dog of my very own. I blamed myself for so much of it. Had I not been so busy drinking that Fourth of July weekend and celebrating with friends, my parents wouldn't have been watching him during that time frame. Had I not been so mouthy, I wouldn't have had a semi-altercation with the man who lived there. Had I not done this/that/etc.….. I could go on and on with how I blamed myself.

When I finally took some time to deep dive into that incident, which, by the way, wasn't until I got sober (I wasn't able to accurately think or evaluate anything in my life until that happened), I really focused on the parts of myself I did not like at that time. I had to get past the action that happened to my dog and focus instead on **ME** and how I acted/behaved following that event. I felt shame with my ability to be a good dog mom because I felt I was immature and did not have my priorities in line. At that time, drinking and partying was my #1 goal. I believed that the only way I could fix the situation was to cause more pain and project more hate because of what was done to me, which was why I was so focused on getting revenge that I thought was needed.

After lots of time, reflection, and tears, I knew that the only way for me to be a better person and a version of myself I was proud of was to eliminate the hate and focus on my own priorities. It was the first time I truly felt like I really was thinking about priorities in my life and how important people/things were to me. Fast forward to today, and I can say I am a next level dog mom. I think about Simon a lot with my current pug, and I do everything I can to make sure I am giving him the best life and as much attention as possible.

And let's not forget to talk about the greatest lesson that the whole experience taught me: the lesson of forgiveness. There's no better way to get past hate than to forgive those who instilled that feeling in you. I've been known to hold grudges and have been revengeful for a big part of my life, and it was always something I did not like in myself. I think that behavior allowed me to avoid really getting deep into the root of why I felt that way.

After the situation with Simon, I did spend quite a bit of time with a therapist, and forgiveness came up often in conversation. I remember in the beginning thinking, "I can never forgive someone who killed my beloved dog."

But…. eventually I did.

There's a great quote Buddha had said that was so applicable to me at this time. He said, "Holding onto anger is like grasping a hot coal with the intent of throwing it at someone else. You are the one who gets burned." Have you ever thought about that quote and how true it is? I was walking around for the better part of **TWO YEARS** angry and hostile at the people who hurt my dog. What good did that do me? Absolutely zero. What did it do to me? It made my soul ugly, my demeanor unpleasant, and my attitude total shit.

I will never forgive that version of Katie, and honestly, I never want to. That version taught me so much and is the reason now I am able to not live in hate. Do people anger me nowadays? Of course. We are human beings, and that is a natural emotion. I no longer have those feelings of hatefulness and nastiness I once did. You anger me, you hurt me, you wrong me, you betray me, a friendship/relationship ends: Okie dokie then. When something gets to that point, I bless and release that person from my life. In the wise words of Tupac, " I still want to see you eat….just not at my table."

That's growth, friends.

Go pour yourself a cup of coffee and sit down and start writing that list of alllllllllll the versions of yourself you can think about. Then get to reverse engineering and find the good in that time to make you better **TODAY** and **TOMORROW**.

Don't forget: give yourself grace and use this exercise to grow. We are not perfect people. No one is. Even at my downright ugliest, heartless, meanest version, I still was a good person with a good heart. I was just a little lost in my way. It is ok to have your shit together while simultaneously driving the Hot Mess Express. Trust me, I've been the conductor of that train for years. We are all a work in progress.

Just like your favorite tv show, Season Twenty is going to be different and more developed than Season One…...

And that is **A-OK**.

Chapter 11
SELF-LOVE SCRIBBLES

Times in my life where I felt awesome, beautiful, incredible, badass, and strong:

Chapter 11
SELF-LOVE SCRIBBLES

Times in my life where I struggled and felt my absolute worst:

Chapter 11
SELF-LOVE SCRIBBLES

Versions of myself through the years (good and bad):

Katie Logic #12:
CATCH FEELINGS FOR YOURSELF

Isn't it crazy how easy it is to catch feelings for another person? Have you ever thought about catching feelings for yourself?

Crazy idea, right?

Friends, you cannot love and live to the best of your ability without first loving your own damn self. Everything….and I mean **EVERYTHING**…. begins with you. You want to talk about becoming confident? It has to start with this right here. It has to start with self-love.

Raise of hands if when you look in the mirror you instantly start picking apart your appearance. Maybe you had a breakout so your skin isn't flawless. Maybe you are having a bad hair day and the curls just aren't doing their thing. Maybe your outfit just makes you feel a little frumpy. Maybe you ate too much cheese and are bloated AF, so you feel meh.

Do you go for the negatives right away? Why as humans do we do this?

Awhile back, I came across an exercise online that said to stand naked in front of a full-length mirror for two minutes every morning and just look at yourself. I took on the challenge to do this, and it was downright **HARD AF** in the beginning to get through those two minutes.   I found myself picking apart absolutely everything about myself. Time took forever to pass, and I think that little bit of boredom made me just go for my own jugular.

I took on this challenge for an entire month, and as the month progressed, I started to noticed I was appreciating my body more and was being kinder to myself. So what if I had a little pooch because I went too hard on gluten that day? I had an enjoyable day with a friend and felt great in the moment, not to mention ate incredible food, so I shouldn't criticize myself for those choices. It was an interesting challenge of self-reflection, appreciation, and self-love.

I challenge you to flip the switch on the mirror roasting of yourself. What about all the amazing things you are looking at in that moment that make you unique and beautiful? Trust me, they are there. You compliment others all the time. Why are you not returning the favor to yourself? How you speak to yourself counts. How you speak about yourself counts. If you've never paid attention to it, now is the time to start. You may not even realize how badly you are critiquing yourself. I think for most people they don't have a clue the amount of negative self-talk they participate in daily.

Think about a time you felt absolutely radiant. Everything was on point, and you just felt absolutely stunning. Maybe you were wearing an outfit that just made you super confident...or your makeup was just perfection...or when you saw a photo of yourself you were like, **"DAYYYUUUUMMMMMMM."** Those are the feelings you want to have every single day. We've got to find that feeling for you, sis!

I get it. It is hard sometimes to appreciate what you are looking at in the mirror when you are already struggling with confidence, especially nowadays with social media setting unrealistic expectations and standards. It is a constant comparison game. Why we allow airbrushed photos and photoshopping and all the edits get to us when we know they are fake is beyond me. It's like society wants us to fall victim to comparison to buy whatever they are trying to sell. Understand that people **LOVE** to see your insecurities and try to capitalize on it for their own selfish reasons.

The moment I decided to love myself was such an empowering moment for me. It was like a switch had been flipped, and I just did not care about anyone else's opinions (revisit Chapter 1 here if needed since everything ties back to FWTT). Instead of pulling out a crop top and talking myself out of wearing it for my home workout where **NO ONE** saw me, I didn't think twice about putting it on and wearing it. Eventually, I started wearing it at the gym or out to shop. Some days my abs were flat and others days I had eaten a ton of gluten and was bloated AF (shout out to my fellow gluten intolerant sisters who know what I mean). It didn't matter. I loved how I felt wearing a crop top, and I embraced **WHATEVER** version of me put it on that day.

There are things that make us feel powerful and confident in our wardrobe, cabinets, and lifestyle. We all have those "power pieces" as I like to call them. If you don't, it's time to figure out what **DOES** make you feel like a **ROCKSTAR** and incorporate that more into your daily life so you can start feeling more confident. In the beginning when I was working on myself and trying to become someone who exuded confidence instead of lacking it, I relied heavily on these power pieces. What were they for me?

My most important one: red lipstick. When I would put this color on I felt like such a badass, and regardless of what the rest of my face/hair/body was doing, I felt **GOOD.** The same red lipstick I wore back then is **STILL** my go to red today. I guess you can say that brand and shade are my signature, and it still makes me feel just as amazing now as it did then.

Other things that made me feel confident and powerful: A victory roll (my favorite hairstyle because I'm low key a 50's housewife trapped in the wrong decade), this killer black pencil skirt I found in the clearance section of a chain department store, and a sky high pair of heels. I also have a form fitting dress that I feel like a straight **BOSS** in when I'm wearing it.

It's not just fancy stuff though. I have a pair of leggings that when I put on I feel like a total superhero when wearing. Anytime I am wearing those items, I feel like I could do anything. As far as style, I loved mixing prints and mismatching. You see a lot of leopard print and tie dye with this one! I always joke with those I train that wearing bright colors, leopard and tie dye makes your workout better, and I stand by that statement, at least for me. Something about being bold brings out the best in me.

So…. I started to wear more of those things and less of the items in my closet that didn't make me feel badass. That pencil skirt? Found a few that were nearly identical and rocked them in different colors. The shoes? Found them in other colors, too. Who cares if I was over six feet tall when I had them on? I felt good being tall. Victory Rolls? In my hair on the regular, even though my mom always reminds me how much she disliked them (Love you, Mom). I also may still wear them since Brett Eldredge once told me in a meet and greet he liked mine since I had one in that day, and I may have a little (i.e. **GINORMOUS**) crush on him. Brett, if you read this, call me!

Then I started to think…..why **DO** I love those things? I loved them because they accentuated aspects that I loved about myself. Pencil Skirts? I loved them because they were long enough to be classy, but tight on my booty. I worked hard for this ass and love it. Victory Rolls? They allowed me to showcase my unique side, and I have always loved being different. They also were a nod to the pinup lifestyle I loved for its artistic appeal, and styling my hair that way allowed me to bring that time frame alive.

The heels? As someone who is tall, I loved that they made me even **TALLER**. When I would wear those suckers I was easily 6'3, and in my mind I looked tough and intimidating even if I wasn't. I loved my height after years and years of feeling like I shouldn't. And mismatched clothing….it just made me feel great because I could combine things I loved and be a little different, which is who I am as a person. To this day my favorite combo is a pair of leopard leggings with a rainbow graphic crop top. The two just make me happy.

If you aren't sure what you love about yourself, think about the things that made you feel freaking amazing and **WHY** they make you feel that way. Start small. I'm not saying you have to throw out your wardrobe and buy all new stuff, but if you know that one pair of leggings makes you feel fierce, why aren't you bringing that fierceness out more than once every so often?

Looking back at that time in my life, you know when I felt the worst about myself and would pick myself apart the most, I wore super baggy oversized stuff and tried to hide. Trust me, when I was seventy+ pounds overweight that was more often than it should've been. I was hiding back then from everything: from myself, from photos, from compliments. **EVERYTHING**. Wearing those kinds of items was a constant reminder of all the things I hated about myself, mostly, that I wasn't confident enough to be me, regardless of size.

Size does not matter, friends. If you are someone who has worked with me or follows me on social media, you know I am all about body positivity and loving your body regardless of what a stupid number on a scale says. Self-love though has to start from within. It has to be **YOU** deciding to love yourself every single day.

Hold up though. What if you have a down day?

Let's face it, everyone will have a day where we feel kind of meh. Does that mean we don't love ourselves? No! Those are the days where we need to love ourselves even more and make sure we are filling our days with words of affirmation or acts of self-love. A down day doesn't mean we can start jumping down the negative self-talk rabbit hole (that used to be my go to move, so I'm well versed on that).

When I find myself having rougher days and maybe some doubt creeps in or there's a lack of motivation or just a feeling of blah, I always start with a solid mirror pep talk. We all know how I feel about affirmations, so I look at myself in the mirror and repeat all the things I am. That pep talk always starts and always ends with, "I am a badass." Sometimes I even need to remind myself that I walked through major battles over the course of my life and have risen from the ashes when so many people counted me out. What I say between those two affirmations in my mirror pep talk depends on the day and what I need some pep with. There's something really soul awakening when you look yourself in the eye and have a stern talking to with yourself.

I've even had days where I write the affirmations on sticky notes and put them up on the mirror to remind myself every time I walk by it what's up. Ya gotta do what ya gotta do. Remember, self-love and finding confidence is a different process for everyone. I cannot stress enough how important it is to find what lights a spark in **YOU** to make both a part of your life.

You know what helps? Throwing a pep rally for yourself…. daily.

If you think back to pep rallies in high school, weren't they the shit? You would get to leave class early and **EVERYONE** would be in hype mode for whatever sport you were having a pep rally for. The energy was contagious, and regardless of the mood you were in when you entered the pep rally, I think it is pretty safe to say you were instantly in a better mood after leaving and ready to carry that positive energy and spirit into the game that night.

This kind of energy…this kind of pep and hype…. you need to be bringing it to yourself every single day. You have to be the greatest hype girl in your life!

It is all about self-love activities, and trust me, you want to have that list of things that you know make you feel good and empower you. My list includes my workout, and I make sure that workout is one that makes me feel super badass and powerful, bubble baths, dancing in my house listening to a killer playlist full of my favorite tunes, sitting in a salt cave, walking my dog, being on the beach, and writing. All of those things **I KNOW** lift my mood and make me feel good. Confidence always ties back to feeling good and finding good. Know what those things are in your life.

Speaking of things that make you feel good….don't love letters make you feel so so so good? I always love getting those sweet messages/texts/notes (shout out to my fellow romantics). I challenge you to write a love letter to yourself. Get in depth with it. Write down all the things you love about yourself. All the things that make you feel amazing. All of the qualities you are proud to have. I don't care if it ends up being twenty pages long. **WRITE THE NOTE TO YOURSELF.**

After you finish this exercise, store it somewhere that you can access and read on a day you may be struggling, on a day you need a reminder how freaking amazing you are. The first time I wrote one, I felt a little silly, and I didn't even get too crazy with it. It was short, maybe only a couple of paragraphs long, but it did get me to a happier mood. A few months later, I threw that letter out (I wish I hadn't in hindsight), and I rewrote it. I thought about all the parts of my body and wrote about as many as I possibly could and what I loved about them. I still have that letter in my desk for a day I may need it.

A line I wrote then that still makes me happy today: "I love my thighs because they are strong…. but also because they can hold a lot of snacks." It's funny because it is true, but that line also makes me happy because I used to hate my thighs. It reminds me of my strength and self-growth.

Have fun with this exercise. Find the good in you and your body and truly **LOVE** every part of it. Don't be afraid to revisit the letter every few months, especially if you are just starting out on your confidence journey.

Promise me something right now in this moment.

Promise me you will love who you are every day, regardless of what crazy version of yourself you may be in that moment. You will love that piece of your journey. Self-love is all about not only loving yourself, but loving the process as you grow every single day. You will **NOT** be afraid of who you are in that moment because **YOU ARE YOU**, and no one should or can change who you are.

And if you are feeling fear on any given day, **PROMISE** me it has nothing to do with the opinion of others….because you already know what I am going to say…..

FUCK WHAT THEY THINK.

Chapter 12
SELF-LOVE SCRIBBLES

What pieces in my wardrobe make me feel powerful and confident?

Chapter 12
SELF-LOVE SCRIBBLES

What are my self-love activities that boost my spirits and make me happy?

CHAPTER 12
SELF-LOVE SCRIBBLES

Use this space to write a love letter to yourself.

BLESS AND RELEASE

Building confidence is full of dealing with the nasty, dirty, really tough stuff. Flowers have to grow through dirt. So do you.

Bless and release in my world is a fancier way of saying "forgive and forget." It goes back to that Tupac quote I shared earlier about wanting others to eat, just not at my table. Blessing and releasing means accepting something you cannot change in your life and making the decision to let it go and no longer hold onto it. It is a decision to move on and take the power back that whatever/whomever stole from you momentarily.

Why do we need to talk about this? It's the one thing that for the beginning part of my confidence journey I did not do. I was working so hard on building up my confidence with things related **TO ME** that I was just pushing some of the things that had impacted me under the rug without properly addressing them. The more I worked on myself, the more I realized that to have confidence, that to feel beautiful, that to be my best self, everything had to start from inside me. Confidence is internal. You could be wearing the most amazing outfit, hair is perfect, makeup flawless, and you still lack confidence if you haven't worked on your confidence muscle.

Think about the fridge. It's plain on the outside, but it's what's on the inside that matters. Right? Well, unless you have one of those super cute retro fridges from the 70s.... you know the ones. Those are incredible on the outside **AND** inside. No one really cares how the outside of the fridge looks, but when you open those doors and see the merriment of snacks and food inside, you get excited. You love it, and then you start to love the fridge in its entirety.

Confidence starts from the inside. You'll never love the outside if you aren't loving the inside. Just like the fridge.

Apologize for making mistakes or hurting someone, but do not apologize for being who you are and making the decision to walk away from something that is harmful to you. We all have had to deal with shitbirds flying around us, trying to shit on our motivation and focus and dreams. They have the choice to speak to you that way; you have the choice to ignore them, walk away, and never give them the time of day again.

Blessing and releasing also means working to let go of any feeling that is negative to you, which also ties back to how you react to the cards you are dealt in life.

My reaction: always to be the good.

I say this statement so much that it is a shocker it isn't tattooed on my body (yet), but it is something that I feel strongly is tied to being not only your confident self, but a happy person, too.

I've mentioned how important self-reflection is, and I have found the best reflections I have done have happened after really awful, soul sucking, challenging times. There's something about being at that rock bottom and broken place where you can just look at your soul and areas of growth so much differently. You are being real, raw, and open to yourself and whatever heartache you are coping with in that moment. There's power in that.

2015 was the year that tried to rob me of all the good when we lost my dad, and losing my grandmothers not long after fueled that feeling so greatly. I spent so much time thinking about life and reflecting on who I was that it led me to realize that I had a chance to keep my loved ones alive by my actions. I don't know about anyone else, but when I suffered these losses I literally would think about every single thing I could about that person. I think a huge part of me was terrified I would **FORGET** things that were so important to me on how they lived, spoke, thought, etc.

When it came to my dad, I would think about his laugh, his sarcastic humor, his unique running gait, his routines for getting ready for work, his motivation, the songs that pumped him up, the way he spoke to others, his mannerisms, etc. I thought about absolutely everything, and I think a big part of me did that to not lose those memories. However, as I was doing that I started to think about the things I loved and respected most about my dad. You guessed it: I made a list of those qualities, and not just for him, but for my grandmothers, my aunt, my uncle, and my good friend Andy, who I had also lost.

Losing someone gives us an opportunity. That opportunity: to bring the things we loved most about the person we have lost back to life. Choose to find the good. Choose to bless and release. Choose to always be better.

Grief comes up a lot with me, and I know it has a tendency to make others uncomfortable. That is okay. I do not care if it makes you uncomfortable, and I know that sounds kind of rude, but the truth is I am not comfortable having to live a life full of grief. Grief entered my life, and I have to choose how I handle it, but that doesn't mean it is something I am comfortable with. Talking about those I have lost and how I have worked through my ongoing obstacles with grief helps me, and that's why I do it and will continue to do so.

Just like your own confidence journey, there is no right or wrong way to approach dealing with grief. What works for one person won't work for another, just like how some of the confidence things we have already discussed may not help you. Of course, I hope they do, but we are all navigating this weird thing called life differently.

I bring that up here because we must also remember not to give up if something doesn't work out as we are trying to improve our confidence and life. You **MUST** put yourself first to work on the habits and skills to make **YOU** better. You **MUST** make the choices to bless and release and move on. What you do **WILL** impact how everything else goes, and only **YOU** know what will help you get to that point.

When it comes to blessing and releasing in your life, I have found this really helps me feel that I have regained control of a situation. I will not let toxicity control me, and I think without acknowledging it, those kinds of things linger and fester. You can't ignore challenging things, situations, or people, because while they may disappear for a bit, they will resurface, and usually they come back stronger than when they left. Choose to deal with them head on so you can find peace with that situation and also within yourself. You cannot move forward while being in limbo.

Release the hot coals. Release the anger. Release the sadness. **CHOOSE** to move forward, not backward.

What do you need to bless and release? Think about the things/people lingering that are currently upsetting you, hurting you so you can come up with a plan of attack to make peace with them.

CHAPTER 13
SELF-LOVE SCRIBBLES

What people/events/things do I currently need to bless and release
from my life?

Katie Logic #14:
QUIT THE COMPARISON GAME FOR GOOD

Real Talk: how many times a day do you scroll social media, go to a store, talk to a person, etc. and immediately start comparing where you are in your life to where someone else is? Multiple times a day? Chances are that was your answer, right?

This is a tough one, friends, and trust me when I say that we have all been there. We are **ALL** guilty of playing the comparison game, and it is by far the most toxic game out there. I know some people will try to say Cards against Humanity is, but no, sis, it definitely isn't.

There was a period of time in my life where I compared absolutely everything I did to something someone else was doing. Ironically, it was when my self-esteem and confidence was the lowest. Coincidence? I think not.

I feel fortunate because at the time when my life was really started to spiral with drinking and bad choices, social media was just starting to be on the up and up. Myspace was phasing out (Bye, Tom), and people were starting to use Facebook and Instagram more. Tik Tok wasn't a thing yet, and a lot of us never hopped onto Twitter at that time.

Present day, all of the social media platforms in existence almost monopolize people's lives, and it can be such a slippery slope. Filters, apps that manipulate how you look, photoshop…. all

165

things that are seen on a daily basis that contribute to the masses becoming insecure or questioning who they are/what they wear/how they do their hair, etc. As a country, we are seeing a rise in so many unhealthy habits and products, younger individuals seeking out things like plastic surgery and Botox, and mental health in a decline. Does that have anything to do with the comparison game that happens on social platforms? **AbsoFUCKINGlutely.**

As someone who has built a successful business using social media, I know it has its benefits. I love the connections I have made through it and the ability I have to positively reach and connect with more individuals. However, just as amazing as it can be, it can be just as devastating and detrimental. If you are someone reading this who is struggling currently with who you are and doom scrolling on social media is only making it worse and contributing to thoughts about self-esteem and self-worth, let's talk, okay?

I had to get really real with myself on social media awhile back, and I advise all of you do the same. We talk about the online trolls in this book, which will unfortunately always be there, and I shared how I had some backlash when I shared my very first before and after photo. Social media can be a harsh and unforgiving place. However, sometimes we are our biggest troll and the worst voice we hear.

I've had to deal with a lot of strange moments with social media in my day, especially as I worked to gain the confidence and self-esteem I have now. From trolls about my weight, to people trying to invade my privacy regarding my divorce and dating life, to an abundance of comments related to my battle with alcohol, to dudes being straight **CREEPS**, to me comparing myself to others, there have been many moments where I thought "Do I even need these accounts?" I am guessing most everyone has had a moment or two like that as well. When that question started to come up in my life, I realized I really needed to set some boundaries with myself regarding social media. How did I do this?

First, and probably one of the hardest for me: I gave myself permission to unplug and **NOT** be active on social media.

My role as an online health and fitness coach is one where I constantly want to be sharing what I am doing regarding my own health and fitness journey, my personal development, my business, etc, and it is a career where that isn't just encouraged, but it is a must. If you aren't showing up on social media, you could be creating issues with the algorithm, you may be missing connections with possible clients, people won't think you are serious, or (insert a slew of other things related to just messing up your business). For the first few years of my business, that's all I would think about when I knew mentally I needed to take a break from scrolling and checking in. I felt like I was failing myself if I didn't, so I kept showing up.

One day I decided I wanted to go to bed early and silenced my phone. It was one of those sleeps that I desperately needed, and one that took me into double digits the next morning. I woke up feeling refreshed and like a brand spanking new woman. Something in that moment told me to just avoid the world that day, so I decided to listen. I completely unplugged, not even logging in to do any of the typical business tasks I would knock out on a Saturday morning. I spent the day focused on self-care, from a long run outside to meal prepping to a bubble bath to cleaning my house. I did not check in online once. It was glorious.

Since that day I have made it a priority to unplug, especially when I feel I need that time for my mental health. If I am having a bad day where I know absolutely everything I am saying is going to come off differently than I intended, I avoid it. If people are just agitating me for no reason, I avoid it. If I have just worked my ass off that week, I avoid it. It was tough at first, but it has been so great from a mental health perspective to be productive in a sense and not on social media. .

Here's the important thing that unplugging does: It allows you to get your mind right, and I think we all know that social media can really mindfuck you if you allow it to. Regardless of your confidence level, if you are feeling down, in a nasty mood, or just very easily agitated, social media is **NOT** the place to go.

I know we think scrolling is mindless and fun and will keep our mind off (insert current brain monopolizing thought here), but it can only make it worse. I found that when I would log in while in that state, my mood and attitude would only spiral. Sure, it is important to be present on social media if you have a business tied to it, but the **MOST** important thing you can do is take care of **YOU** first. If not, anything that is going to happen on social media is going to be mediocre at best or just bring your mood down. Besides, chances of you running a business that requires 24/7 operation is probably pretty unlikely. Every business has standard business hours. Make sure you make some for yourself, too.

Can't unplug?

I feel like everyone can and no one has to be logged in constantly, but if you truly can't, then evaluate what it is that you are a) hoping to gain from social media that day b) hoping to add or accomplish on social media that day or c) the sense of urgency related to whatever you think you need to do. In my own experience, I felt like I had to do this and had to do that because social media experts were telling me the key times to post during the week, and if I missed them then I was screwing myself over. When I really sat down to think about it, nothing was so pressing it had to be done that day. It can wait. Make a to do list and get to it when you can the next day.

I am at a point now where there is usually one day a week where I unplug, and some days I am feeling absolutely great. You don't have to be a cranky pants to need to avoid social media. Some days the sunshine and beach may just be calling, and you want to make memories instead of scroll. Your world, your rules, sis.

The second thing I did regarding boundaries and social media: I started setting a timer. I bought a really cute one on Amazon and if I knew I had work that needed accomplished on social media, I set it with a specific time. When that timer went off, I was done with that for the day. Was it effective for me? Absolutely.

Here's why it worked for me: social media is a vortex, a time suck. I may tell myself I am logging into the Facebook to message a few potential clients, then next thing I know I'm scrolling through an album of a friend of a friend's dog's birthday party. Don't even get me started on how times flies when you are scrolling through Tik Toks. It is sooooo easy to fall off course without a plan, and I was guilty as charged of doing that. Having a timer allowed me to be focused and productive, and I needed that.

The unfollow/unfriend option was something else very critical to the boundaries I established on social media, and if you are someone struggling with the comparison game, I cannot stress how important it is. Back when I first started online coaching, it was thing to add as many friends as possible to help network and connect. As someone not super into social media at the time, I would do the things I saw other top coaches do on YouTube videos and training videos. However, I was getting started with the business aspect while also trying to focus on my own health and fitness journey, improve my self-esteem and opinion of myself, and really trying to maintain a sober lifestyle. I had a lot going on.

Social media to me back then really fucked with my head. I would log in and see someone's fitness progress and instantly try to cut myself down because I wasn't at that point yet. I saw someone hitting a business milestone I hadn't hit yet and considered myself a failure. I would see people going places and get upset I wasn't invited or included. It was comparison after comparison after comparison. Barf!

A little digression here....and another plug for personal development.... if you are comparing yourself, dig deep and figure out what the issue is. Is it body image? Business oriented? A feeling of abandonment? Once you identify the root of the issue, there's the topic to focus on when picking out your next PD book. Make a list, search for books or podcasts related to that or ask for recommendations, and start working on improving yourself from the inside out.

When that comparison stuff was going on with me, I really battled a lot of demons with it for a while. I think the most important thing to know about that is that it is **NORMAL** to compare. We all do it, but back at that point I felt like an awful person for the feelings I had. It all came back to my lack of confidence and feeling of self-worth. I was working so hard to improve my overall health and build a thriving business, and because of the way our society is, I wanted all of that overnight.

So…. I put on my blinders and stayed in my lane. I unfollowed or hid people's posts that would make me feel a certain way as I was working on building myself up. It was nothing against them and nothing they did; this was all me and how I reacted to their social media posts. I still tend to hide people on social media. It has nothing to do with a confidence thing anymore, but more about triggers in other areas, like politics, religions, policies, etc. Bottom line: if it isn't helping me grow positively, I don't want to see it. Don't be afraid to hide people. They won't know, and you can work on building up yourself to no longer care what they put up. I'm sure many have hidden or blocked my stuff over the years, and that is ok with me. Do you, boo!

One thing that also was incredibly important to me on social media was being a positive light. Life is not all sunshine and roses, we know that, but there was that time in my life where I literally would try to get into every fight and debate that I saw on social media. Why, Katie? What good did that do for you? Absolutely nothing. It burnt bridges, it made me look stupid for sure, and I always regretted how the conversations would end up.

To be honest, when I drank this was **MUCH** worse, because I was such a loose cannon then. Man, do I cringe just thinking back about some of the debates I would get myself into back in the good 'ol days. Let's be real, too…. I was drinking heavily, and many of these internet fights I don't even remember taking place. That's probably a good thing because I know they were super cringe. Taking a moment right now to pat myself on the back for the personal growth and strides I have made since then.

Negativity breeds negativity, and we all see that on social media every day. I made a very conscientious decision to not partake in that kind of that dialogue because it added no value to my life. Instead, I wanted to focus on spreading the love, positivity, and sunshine in my heart that I knew many needed.

Know this: If you are not part of the solution, you are part of the problem. I know that is harsh, but that is just the stone-cold truth. We are living in a negative, cruel, and unkind world. If you are contributing to things/discussion/activities that fall in those areas, you are part of the problem. I was a part of the problem for a long time, and I know it. I participated in those kinds of discussions and am not innocent at all. We've all been there. The difference: are you staying there or moving forward in a positive way to help others and make a difference? I am choosing to make a difference. It starts with a positive, kind, open heart.

Social media can bring out the worst in people, yes, but it also can bring out the best. I know it has connected me to so many people who can relate to things I have gone through, and I have been able to help motivate or inspire them in some way, just as many of you have helped me in the same way.

Moral of the story with social media: determine what you want to get out of it, don't let it consume your life, and never, ever let it dictate what you should or shouldn't do. There are a lot of highlight reels out. Make sure you remember that anyone can share whatever they want in a filtered picture. None of that is tied to your worth, your value, or your unique amazingness. Follow and befriend people who make you feel good and add to your quality of life. If they are dimming your light in any way, time to unplug from them. We only shine bright over here, honey.

Chapter 14

SELF-LOVE SCRIBBLES

How are you currently playing the comparison game? Do a social media audit to determine if those you following are adding to this.

Katie Logic #15:
REMEMBER WHO THE HELL YOU ARE

Sometimes you just need to look in the mirror and realize that you are the person who is holding you back. **YOU.** You can blame others for their opinions of you, their comments, the trollish DMs, yadda yadda yadda.… but it all comes down to **YOU** and how badly you want to be happy and confident for **YOU.** It's You vs You….always.

"Shut your damn donut hole, Katie."

That's what I tell myself at any point in time where I start questioning something, giving more than a second's thought to some dumb ass rude comment someone made that has me thinking something crazy, or letting someone else get in the way of my good mood.

You need to start saying that, too. Do **NOT** let anything negative come out of that beautiful mouth of yours. You have worked too hard on your confidence to this point or **ARE IN THE PROCESS** of working on your confidence to allow **YOU** to be the person to send you back where you started. Sometimes you are the most confident human being on the planet. You know your worth, you know what you stand for, yet you still will hit road bumps and obstacles that will challenge that. Life will always be throwing some kind of shitstorm your way.

There will always be trolls popping up, always setbacks, always things to make you question what you are doing or where you are at in your current situation. There's always going to be something coming at you and coming for you, so grab that umbrella and walk into that storm knowing you can take it on and walk out of it appreciating the rainbow that we all know is waiting at the other side.

Friends, you will constantly have things pop up in your life to challenge you. There are days where I feel like every single moment something new is jumping out at me forcing me to think and reevaluate. Hi, life.

You should never be afraid to take on a challenge or obstacle when it pops up, and with time and confidence, I hope you realize that you can weather any storm that comes at you. I used to be so fearful, and every confrontation or slightly negative situation left my stomach in knots and me losing sleep. That's back during the old Katie days though…. aka the days where I didn't know who I was, what I had to offer, and what I was capable of accomplishing. Back then I thought the smallest things were the end of the world.

Have you ever sat down to think about some of the shitstorms you've walked through in your day? You've been through some pretty tough stuff without a doubt….and you've made it here. You've survived those tough days, you've taken from them, and regardless of what they were, you were **FORCED** to grow from those moments. Every single one of us has seen our own storms, yet we have been able to get through them.

There have been moments in my life that I truly did not think I would survive. Thinking back to some of them, I just feel the pain and struggles I felt then. I remember those early days after losing my dad when I didn't know if would I ever be able to laugh again. I remember thinking I would never be able to leave my mom's side, that I would need to be there to take care of her as she went through her own broken journey that I couldn't possibly understand. As I started out on my sober journey, I remember being terrified that I would never be included in fun events again, or that I didn't know when/if I would fall off the wagon and start drinking again. I remember so many things about that time that made where I am at today seem impossible. It always seems impossible until it is done.

As those tough times come at you, I challenge you to think about some of the things we have discussed already. How are you reacting? What are you taking from that situation? How are you treating others? I knew then and I knew now that I just really wanted everything I did to be rooted in kindness and love. After all, you are only as pretty as how you treat people, and nothing shows your true soul like how you treat others when you are broken down and at rock bottom. Kindness is free, and while it may burn zero calories, the impact it has on your overall health and the health of others is immeasurable.

I realized a big lesson a long time ago that I have shared with many of you who I have been fortunate enough to know in the real world, and it is this: You must be willing to celebrate your failures as much as you celebrate the triumphs in life. You must not be ashamed of the scars life has given you. The wound may be closed or it may be fresh, but it is there to serve as a reminder that you are a warrior. You got through something hard, and whether they are external or internal where only you can see them, you know they are there.

My scars are symbolic of my strength. They make me **ME**. They have given me the gift of knowing I can get through hard times and I will always push through those hard moments. Life may throw those shitstorms and setbacks your way, but it is up to you to turn that setback into a beautiful comeback story. We all love a good comeback.

Everything comes back to belief in yourself…

Belief in who you are.
Belief in what you have to offer others and the world.
Belief that you deserve happiness and an amazing life.

We all have something to offer. We are all unique and powerful in our own way. Isn't that an incredible thought? We all bring something special to this world. For many of us, it is just forgetting what others think/say/suggest and just getting to know who we are and living the life we truly want for ourselves.

Whenever a shitstorm comes my way, I have an attack plan, which is made up of some non-negotiables in my life. Think about where you work. If a tornado touched down while you were at work, there is a plan on what to do to stay safe, right? You need to have a plan in place for when the weather gets rocky in your life, too.

Some of the things you need to incorporate into your plan are probably already showing on the lists you have made if you have been doing that as you read this book. What are the things that make you happy and bring you joy? What brings you peace? What helps you re-center and regain control of your life?

My non-negotiables when life gets rocky:

First and foremost, I unplug from social media. This was something that for a long time I avoided because I thought I couldn't. As a business owner, that essentially meant I was closing up shop for the day, as my clients wouldn't be responded to, those wanting to order or connect would get ignored, and I wasn't "showing" up to continue to motivate or coach them. I got to thinking about it though, and most businesses are not open 24/7. I did not need to be. Unplugging allows me to set those much-needed boundaries so I can be **BETTER** for those I serve through my business. When life is a little rough, I take a few days off. I don't ghost people; I share that I won't be accessible and will get back to them soon. Taking care of me has to come first.

Next up, I fill my cup. I fill it up with the things that make me feel my best. I take a long bubble bath with a good book. I put on my favorite face mask. I snuggle with my dog. I make a cup of my favorite coffee. I make sure I do a workout that makes me feel like a badass. I get outside and enjoy nature. I put on my favorite 80's jams and dance around my house. And I eat like a fucking trash panda…. which means I am hitting up my favorite local pizza shop and donuts.

Then…. I reflect. How is what is happening impacting me on a day to day basis? Once I identify that (what up, list #4000), I start thinking of what I need to do to spin it into something positive to not take it as a setback. Sometimes that is easy to do; Other times I cry a lot, and it takes days to figure out the "what's next" puzzle.

What I don't do? Sweep it under the rug and not attack it head on. That's the only way I am able to move on. I remind myself I'm a fucking boss bitch, and I've got this. Ignoring something and letting that fester stage happen will only start impacting your mental health and challenging your confidence, self-worth, and outlook. Don't let it do that.

This is your reminder that fucking up is part of life. Sadness, grief, and loneliness will have a part in it, too. You can choose to let that define you or empower you to be better, happier, healthier, and stronger. The choice is yours.

As my mother always says, "Life is not for sissies." It sure as shit isn't. You will always have obstacles thrown at you. You will always have people doubting you or making you question your worth, and you will always have those shitstorms. You will have moments where you may revert back to less than confident ways. You will go through breakups and friendships ending and hard times. Welcome to being human. It **WILL** happen. It happens to all of us, even the most confident.

What do you do when this happens?

You take a minute to get those emotions out. Cry like a baby. Stay in bed until 2pm…. whatever it takes. Then you put on your big girl panties and pull yourself together. You put on something that makes you feel confident like we discussed earlier. You do something that brings you joy.

During a few recent rough spots in my life, I added something to my coping routine. One of my new go to moves is having a cereal party. Don't know what that is? Go buy a bunch of different kinds of cereal and just crush the different kinds for days. These parties are best with severe bedhead and oversized sweatpants you may or may not have been wearing for days. So what if it is loaded with sugar…. sometimes you've got to do what you've got to do.

You look in the mirror, remind yourself of what a badass you are, say **FUCK WHAT THEY THINK** out loud maybe a time or ten, then you bless and release that shit.

I think it is so important to appreciate the emotions you go through and truly honor them…. which sounds weird to say, but you need to go through them to **GROW** through them.

Feeling those emotions and going through those stages does not mean you are weak or lack confidence. You are taking back the **POWER** of the situation. Have you ever thought about it like that? All too often we give a situation, a thing, a person **POWER** that makes us feel a certain way, and then we allow that power to control us. **YOU** are in control of how you attack your life and what you allow to wreck you. You vs You, remember?

Think about something that scares you right now…. maybe it is a class at the local gym. You really want to get active, you have been wanting to go forever.... but you are scared. **WHY**? You have given that class–that little sixty-minute opportunity for you to sweat and get better—all the power, and that has kept you from giving it a shot. Take away the power it has. It is **JUST** a class. Maybe you won't even like it. What if you did? We give too many things and people power that prevent us from being our absolute best self.

I've shared many times on social media how important it is to pep talk yourself. I don't care how silly it seems or feels, sis, if no one is going to pep talk you, you be your biggest cheerleader and remember **WHO THE HELL YOU ARE**. I'll stand in front of my huge selfie mirror and talk to myself to build up my confidence and spirits. I will put on a killer playlist that makes me feel powerful AF. I will hang up notes around my house with reminders of things I am proud of or things I love about myself. Sometimes you need to up that dose of self-love and take it to the next level. No better time to do that than when you feel like you are losing yourself a bit and giving power to something or someone else.

I know who I am. I know I am extra and over the top and loud and extroverted and foul mouthed. I know I am cynical and sometimes a poor communicator who hides her feelings from others. I know I am not perfect, but I do know I am perfect for someone out there, and I know I am a good human with a great heart who doesn't need to change a thing for anyone. I will not dim my light because I am too bright for someone else. I will not water myself down to make myself more digestible to others. If I am too much for you to swallow, I'm going to let you go ahead and choke. I will be me, this weird yet magical human being, and love who I am regardless of what may be happening in my life. Self-love is the most important love. Without it you can't truly love anything to the best of your ability.

I am enough.
You are enough.
Let's promise each other right now we will not forget that, regardless of what life throws at us.

WE hold the power in our own two hands. Do **NOT** allow someone or something to take it from you.

Giving you a fist bump virtually right now because we've got this.

Chapter 15

SELF LOVE SCRIBBLES

Brain dump the times you were forced to grow through what you went through. What failures have happened in your life to make you better today? What scars exist to remind you of how strong you are?

Chapter 15
SELF-LOVE SCRIBBLES

What is your attack plan if a life shitstorm comes your way?

SHUT YOUR DONUT HOLE

Your life isn't yours if you always care what others think.

Take a second to let that sink in.

If you are living your life based on what others want for you or how they think you should live it, it's their life. You are living a life for **THEM.** You aren't bringing main character energy to that. Sis, you are on the sidelines. Regain control of the narrative and be in control, even if that seems like you are being over the top, extra, annoying, or whatever adjective comes to mind. You will also always be too much of something for someone. This is your reminder that those who say you are too much **AREN'T** your people.

If you've ever worked in sales you may have had to do a thirty second or sixty second sales pitch or something similar. It's your elevator pitch aka the chance to tell people what they need to know about you in a short time. My time in higher education had me doing these often when I changed jobs, and I always thought they were weird, but now I see them as such an effective hiring method. You have to have a solid sense of who you are, what you have to offer, and what sets you apart from anyone else in the room.

I challenge you to think of what you would include in yours, because those are the qualities you hopefully love most about yourself and are the proudest of. They are the things that make you shout from the rooftops with joy.

If I had to make one? It probably would go something like this:

"I'm not afraid of the hard talks, the confrontations, or anything that can help me grow and develop as a person. I work incredibly hard, and am a straight forward, blunt individual, sometimes to a fault. I am ridiculous, I love donuts, sequins, and Little Debbie Christmas Tree Cakes more than most, and I have zero shame in how I live my life and things. If I love you, I will love you with every fiber of my being and my whole heart. If you are in my life, I will be loyal to a fault and do everything I can to protect you, support you, and make you laugh. I will always share my sparkle and do everything in my power to make **EVERY SINGLE PERSON** I meet feel like a somebody.

It has taken me over three decades to realize that it is **OKAY** if not everyone likes me. I get it. I'm loud sometimes, and that bothers people. I cuss a lot, my sense of humor may be deemed to be inappropriate, and that may make some people cringe a little. I talk about wrestling more than most, I really love eyelashes, and I am always always always hunting down a donut to smash. I either go all in or I don't go at all. That goes for my work, that goes for relationships, that goes for just how I live my life. I don't know how to half ass, I only full ass. I know sometimes I intimate others with my boldness, and because of that some people have labeled me a bitch. I don't need validation from anyone, and that makes people uncomfortable at times. I will **ALWAYS** be too much for some people out there, and someone will always be asking me to "tone it down," and that is okay, because at the end of the day I'm enough for me, and that's all that matters."

Go make one for yourself. Right now, don't even think about it. Pretend there is no time limit…. just ramble off all the things you love most about life and who you are. What makes you **YOU**????

I am a lot to handle, yes, I know. You may be, too. But here's the thing….

I know who I am. That's really where confidence comes from. Confidence comes from knowing and appreciating all the things that radiate from within and that make you different from the person next to you. I'm not for everyone, and I don't want to be. It's taken me a long ass time to realize that, but once I did, life became easier and more comfortable for me. As you sit down and write out your list and work on your elevator pitch, you may write something down that makes you think…"Hmm, maybe I shouldn't write that or say that." Nah, that's exactly something you should include. This is about **YOU** acknowledging who you are and embracing all the bold, weird, unique things that make you **YOU**.

Know what else it has taken me over three decades to realize?

The right people will love you for who you are.
The right people will never ask you to change.
The right people will never prefer a watered down "safe" version of who you are.
The right people will embrace your weird, authentic, crazy self **AS IS**.

And if they don't like you for you, **FUCK THEM**.

A few final thoughts and reminders as we wrap up our time together here....

It is possible to be the shit without shitting on anyone. I think some people tend to forget that. As much as I hope you take away some valuable nuggets from this book to help you on your confidence and self-discovery journey, I also really hope you take some things that remind you to just be a good person. Just because someone's light is different than yours doesn't mean it is better or worse. Cheer them on. Applaud them. Appreciate their differences. Learn from them. And, by all means, please don't try to dissuade them, discourage them, or cut them down just because their path looks different than what you took in life.

People will read this book and either love it or hate it, and that's totally fine. **BUT**.... what I hope everyone realizes as they turn the last page is that there no **ZERO** reason to be the kind of person who steps on others to get ahead. I mean, is a queen really a queen if her throne is placed on top of all those she has stepped on, smothered, and smashed to get there? Nah, girl. That's no queen.

Do you realize we can all be the shit.... like **ALL OF US**?????

I don't know who ever felt that there was a cap on how many people could be the shit, but I am here to tell you there isn't one. Let's just all enter into some kind of pact right now to be the shit.

I do not come with a dimmer switch, and neither should you. So if I am too extra, too much, or too (insert whatever here) for you, know it is ok. I like myself. Your like is just extra, and that's all it will ever be. Remind yourself of that daily. You don't **NEED** likes if you already like who you are. If someone tells you that what you do is too bright or too anything, suggest that they get sunglasses because you are **NOT** dimming who you are for **ANYONE**. Please adopt that mentality because I can guarantee you that someone will approach you at some point to tone it down, calm down, chill out, whatever . That's just life.

This is your reminder that you are **YOU**. There is no one on this planet like you, and that is pretty freaking amazing. Shine bright, sis. It is ok if people don't like you or want you in their life. It is okay if you are too much for someone. They may not be your people, but they are doing you a favor and making room for those who **DO** want a seat at your table and in your life. Do not water down who you are just because someone else can't handle you as you are.

NEVER.

This is a formal invitation (with glitter and a super Katie-like artistic font) to be you.

Wear the clothes that make you happy.
Say the things you want to say.
Do the things you want to do.
Set the boundaries you need to set.
Match the energy you want to match.
Love who and what sets your soul on fire.
Eat the things that you love (especially donuts).
Be you! You are a magical person!

You can be a walking enigma and make people scratch their heads.

You can be confident AF but also have some insecurities that you are actively working on overcoming.

You can be strong AF but also be soft.

You can be ambitious as all heck but like to take three days off in a row.

You can feel sexy in a sequin dress and also in baggy sweatpants and no bra.

You can value your health but sometimes eat donuts for every meal.

You don't have to make sense to anyone as long as you make sense to **YOURSELF!**

Do me a favor and release the idea that there is a "perfect" way to be. We are all imperfectly perfect just doing our best every single day. There will be magnificent days, there will be hard days, but regardless of what kind of day it is, promise me one final thing....

You will love yourself, whatever version of you shows up that day.

This confidence journey may be just beginning for you, but know you will get there. Review the lists you made during our time together in these pages. Review them often. Change them up as your life changes. Be a work in progress **ALWAYS** when it comes to your confidence, and don't stop working on it one day because that day you felt amazing. That confidence muscle **MUST** be worked every single day!

If anyone tries to make you feel/be/do anything that doesn't feel right, tell them to shut their donut hole. Say it with confidence, say it loudly and proudly, and say it with a smile on your face. Then…. proceed to enjoy the tastiest sprinkle donut you can find and celebrate the fact that you have released the desire to please other people and live your life how others think you should.

Congrats on becoming free to be your magical and best self, sis. I'm raising a donut in your honor and giving you an aggressive high five through these pages. You did it.

I'M SO FUCKING PROUD OF YOU.

ACKNOWLEDGEMENTS

It is so hard to sit down to shout out all of the people who have helped me and supported me on this journey. There have been so many that I could devote an entire book just to praising you for your support, motivation, and love! Know that I appreciate you all more than I could ever put into writing.

First of all, I need to shout out the people who really deserve a standing ovation, and that would be all my haters and the dead plants that were once a part of my life. I would've never gotten to the place I am right now had it not been for you. For every person who ever doubted me, who talked shit on me, who made fun of me, who tried to cut me down, who called me names, and who tried to be an energy vampire in my life....**THANK YOU** from the bottom of my heart. You made me stronger, you made me realize who I was, you made me grow as a person, and you made me better.

Of course, I have to thank my parents, the two most supportive people I have ever known. While my dad may not be on this Earth to read this book, I know he has been with me every step of the way, and I know he is proud of me for finally making this dream a reality. It is because of him that I fell in love with writing, it is because of him that I refuse to give up on myself, and it is because of him I am a foul mouthed, yet snarky individual. I know right now he is cheering for me just as loudly as when our Cubbies won the World Series.

My mother continues to be my biggest cheerleader and the best friend I could ever ask for, and I am so thankful for her unwavering support regardless of what crazy thing I tell her I am going to do. Thank you for loving me at every weird stage of my life, and most importantly, thank you for raising me in a way where I could be my genuine self without any judgment. I don't know what I would do without your wisdom, support, and love. You are the greatest mother and woman on the planet, and I love you so fucking much!

To my brother, who took the blame for so many of my actions when we were younger but still loves and cheers me on anyway, thank you. We may be polar opposites of each other, but I am so thankful the world has allowed me to have a brother like you to balance out my craziness in our family. Let's celebrate with some sugar water.

To my incredible friends who make up so many different friend circles in my life.... thank you for being on this journey with me. To Kelly and JPG, you guys have been with me since I was in preschool and have literally been through the thick of it with me. Not one good or bad thing has happened in life without you guys being a part of it. We will always be friends....you guys know too much.

To my partner in crime Erika aka Mary, I'm not sure what I would do without you or our friendship. I may have thought you were a royal bitch the first time we met, but you are truly a sister to me who has had my back through some **SHIT**. Thanks for always pulling me out of it and always being down for donuts, especially during the creation of this book.

To all of my other friends who I could never possibly list…. thank you, thank you, thank you. To late night phone calls to endless laughter to brunch dates to trips to sitting with me as I ugly cried to wellness checks, you all have loved me for who I really am and have given me so much support through all the ups and downs. I know I am surrounded by the best humans when no one even bats an eyelash when I do something extra or weird. You all are truly an extension of my family, and I am forever grateful for you.

Finally, to Hanson Gregory, the man who claims to have invented the donut back in 1847, thank you for punching a hole in some dough and bringing us this glorious delight. Not all heroes wear capes. Some make donuts.

katie kramer

is a health and wellness coach, group fitness instructor, motivator, and author. She currently lives in Virginia Beach and is always on the hunt for an amazing donut.

🌐 www.thesparklefitnessbabe.com

@sparklefitnessbabe

@sparklefitnessbabe